School Administrator's Guide to Flexible Modular Scheduling

Alexander M. Swaab

Illustrations
by
Judith Bleda Yager

Parker Publishing Company, Inc.
West Nyack, New York

© 1974, *by*

PARKER PUBLISHING COMPANY, INC.

West Nyack, New York

Library of Congress Cataloging in Publication Data

Swaab, Alexander M
  School administrator's guide to flexible modular
scheduling.   74-5616
    Bibliography: p.
    1. Schedules, School.   I. Title.
LB1038.S88   371.2'42   73-14732
ISBN 0-13-792473-9

Printed in the United States of America

School Administrator's Guide
to Flexible Modular Scheduling

This book is dedicated to
Paul Preuss, Principal
and
Robert Palmer, Director of Guidance
Norwich Senior High School

for their dedication to youth and their commitment to the field of public education. Also
for making possible the five most exciting and
fruitful years of my professional career.

About the Author

ALEXANDER M. SWAAB has had a wide range of experience in teaching, special education, vocational training and public school administration. He was principal of Norwich Senior High School, Norwich, N.Y. for five years during which time the school transformed from a traditional program to one of the first schools in New York State to adapt the Flexible Modular Schedule. He has been an I/D/E/A Fellow, a speaker at the National Association of Secondary School Principals, and the New York State Association of Secondary School Principals and has consulted widely with schools interested in the areas of Flexible Scheduling, Learning Activity Packages and other areas of secondary school curriculum development.

Foreword

This book progresses from an overall view of traditional schedules to the concept of Flexible Modular Scheduling, to the actual mechanics of creating FMS, to problems of institutional change, and, finally, to evaluation and research. In each section, the author provides basic, informative material to illustrate his points by drawing from his own and his faculty's experience at the Norwich (New York) Senior High School.

In addition to the "how to" information this book deals with, there is, in my judgment, an equally important thread that runs through it. In essence, this thread is an appeal to school people to risk a new era in educational life. The problem is not one of merely introducing, for example, a new science program. Quite the contrary: the author is suggesting a radical restructuring of the relationships that exist between administrators and teachers, among teachers, between teachers and students, and among students. Such a restructuring will not come easily. The critical questions are not of mechanics but of attitudes. And the most important attitude to be changed is the one that deals with how teachers and administrators see youngsters in schools—as passive or resistant recipients of teacher input or as potentially active learners who are seeking satisfaction of their learning needs. The author with his proposal for Flexible Modular Scheduling obviously comes down on the "active learners" side with all the risk this entails.

Does it take a particular kind of principal to induce the kind of change which is the focus of the book? Though I have no hard data by which to answer the question, I think the response has to be in the affirmative. Primarily, my observations of the Norwich situation and others with which I have been associated suggest that the change-oriented principal needs to be assertive, not passive; risk-taking, not cautious; open to feedback, not closed. In addition, this principal needs to see the maintenance of the system as only a means to an end, not an end in itself as is so often the case.

Finally, as I reflect on the book, I think that Alex Swaab is really issuing an invitation to school principals to join him in a very exciting adventure that has big pay-offs for youngsters in school, for teachers, and for administrators. The system that the book describes *works*. It is not without problems, both in its development and its operation. But problems or not, FMS as it is described in the book is a far cry from the sterile structure that characterizes most high schools today—and in the day when most of the readers of this book were in high school. My reactions to school life under FMS are that it would be fun to be a student in that kind of a school.

Arthur Blumberg
Professor of Education
Syracuse University

A Word from the Author

Flexible Modular Scheduling is one of the most significant and rapidly spreading educational innovations since the high school became the cornerstone of American secondary education at the turn of the 20th century. In 1963 there were eight schools that field-tried the new program. Today it is estimated that well over 2,000 public and private secondary schools in the country are using this form of scheduling. Each year the number of schools moving to the adoption of this schedule increases significantly.

Flexible Modular Scheduling is being adopted because of its important program implications. Based on the implementation of the Trump Plan, Flexible Scheduling has resulted in the dynamic and creative restructuring of the secondary school's organization while still keeping ties with the basic principles of American public education. It has been a cogent answer to the critics of traditional education, in that it allows the school to increase its options for program development while substantially reorganizing the curriculum and teacher/pupil meeting patterns in a more efficient manner. Team teaching, individualized instruction, independent study, small grouping and the development of individual student responsibility can all be systematically programmed through the proper organization of the schedule.

The dissemination of practical information about this vital new program remains inadequate and incomplete. Early books in the field have quickly become dated and are often misleading in their information. This is unfortunate because the powerful forces put into motion by the new scheduling have captured the imagination of educators at all levels from coast to coast.

This book offers the reader an up-to-date, practical review of Flexible Modular Scheduling. It provides a comprehensive overview as well as a complete guide to developing an administrator designed, manually constructed master schedule.

Several chapters are devoted to a detailed explanation of the tools of scheduling, telling where to begin in schedule design and explaining all the necessary data in practical terms so the reader will know how to design a master schedule. The mechanics of making such a schedule are applicable in the small rural school as well as in the large urban school. The manually designed master schedule is especially useful for schools that cannot afford the expensive commercialized computer programs or are dissatisfied with their performance and are looking for a viable alternate.

The approach is eclectic and borrows from many sources. The reader will be able to relate and adapt the concepts and procedures described in this book to his own local situation. Practical suggestions are given on how to work with students during their unstructured or independent study time—an important topic for all those contemplating or already in a flexible schedule. A review of the literature on school evaluations is offered with specific references and assistance for the administrator in interpreting the program to the public. Special value is drawn from Norwich Senior High School, New York, used here as a model to look at and learn from as it went through the change process from a traditional school to a school deeply involved in the extensive changes flexible scheduling permits.

A special section is devoted to institutional change, since the transformation of a school from one operating level to another requires new skills that the administrator needs to acquire. The institutional change process is outlined in terms of the basic framework required, and augmented with a step-by-step analysis of the actual activities leading to successful restructuring. This is valuable because so often the administrator is confronted with wanting to make a change in the institution but not having the expertise to manage the process.

The book is written and directed to the individual who needs both a good "grounding" in the ABC's of Flexible Modular Scheduling and the school administrator who would like to use the administrator-designed FMS schedule.

Alexander M. Swaab

Acknowledgments

The author spent two years working with the Norwich faculty in the preparation of the program. Many leading schools were visited throughout the United States in an effort to find the best format to use in scheduling Norwich Senior High School. He has also worked extensively as a consultant with other schools in helping them establish their programs and looks with satisfaction at the number of schools adopting this administrator designed, flexible modular schedule.

As with all major endeavors, a number of people played key roles in helping to bring the program about. Special thanks are extended to the Board of Education of the City of Norwich, New York, for its willingness to create an environment in which effective change could take place. Also acknowledgment is made to Ivan Hunt, Norwich Superintendent of Schools, and Dr. Richard Mace, former Assistant Superintendent for Instruction, for making available the key resources to see the job done well. Without a doubt the reason the reorganization in Norwich worked so well was that the community was fortunate in having a faculty dedicated and committed to the interests of youth. About this particular faculty, it could truly be said that "those who dare to teach must never cease to learn."

On a more personal level, special appreciation is extended to Pat Maynard and Kay Spenard for their labors in preparation of the manuscript.

CONTENTS

9. Evaluating the Program in a Flexible Modular
Schedule *(cont.)*

dent study and use of unstructured time • Absenteeism and tardiness • Drop-out rate • Achievement testing • Regents pupil questionnaires • Parental survey • Faculty survey • Summary

Scheduling time chart • Definitions of terminology • Westinghouse scheduling contract • Developing the course configuration: a faculty packet • An evaluation report on the modular schedule of Northeast High School, St. Petersburg, Florida • Four-year comparative study at Norwich Senior High School • Bibliography

School Administrator's Guide
to Flexible Modular Scheduling

1

Developing a Solid Foundation
for the Flexible Modular Schedule

With the rapid rate of curricular
change, team teaching, interdisciplinary learning, continuous progress
programs and student liberalization policies sweeping schools, the need to
work within a structure that permits the management and professional
staff as well as the students the greatest number of options may be the
key factor to success. It is for this reason that Flexible Modular
Scheduling is gaining such wide acceptance. FMS is not a specific program
but rather a method of organization—implemented through scheduling—
which dramatically increases the school administrators' options for developing and initiating a wide range of program reform. However, simply
adopting the schedule cannot guarantee that the changes will take place
or happen successfully.

The new method of scheduling will address itself to some major areas of
weakness in the traditional schedule and it goes a long way to hurdling the
road blocks to school innovation present in a more conventional schedule.
It is in this spirit, we believe, that a school must study and explore the
feasibility of FMS. A move to FMS is not a panacea for all educational
problems at the secondary level. If, instead, it is viewed as an evolutionary
move to make possible a stronger and more viable school program it will
be more realistic and, ultimately, more productive.

REASONS FOR ADOPTING A MODULAR SCHEDULE

Basically, there are seven reasons for moving to a FMS. These include:

1. The desire to arrange for *variable time blocks* for different classes and on separate days.
2. The creation *variable instructional patterns* such as large group, labs, regular class, small groups, or individualized instruction.
3. The *weighting of courses* on a varying basis using the amount of time allocated to each course as a determining factor.
4. Permitting students greater selection of courses.
5. Making available unstructured time in the school day for a student to engage in independent study.
6. Increasing the program alternatives and options for the school.
7. Breaking the monotony of the traditional schedule.

Each of these objectives for moving to the new type of schedule will be discussed.

1. Variable Time Blocks

Traditionally, time blocks in school run from 40 to 55 minutes in length, with between six to eight blocks in a school day. Almost all courses meet for a "period" once a day, five times a week. (See Figure 1-1.) Since the same amount of time is allocated for each period there is nothing to suggest that there is any relationship between the unit of time and the curriculum to be taught in the course. If you asked the personnel from a school that used a 40-minute time period, they would tell you that 40 minutes was the optimum amount of time to run courses. In another school using a 50-minute time period, the personnel would argue that 50 minutes was exactly right for the program in that school. The truth is that there is no single unit of time that is an optimum amount applicable to all areas of the school curriculum. The basis for a single time unit in schools is purely historical, with no educational foundation or justification. Not only do the demands for time vary between different subject matter courses, but different teaching techniques in the same course may require different time requirements from day to day. For all too long the element of time was considered a constant in the school scheduling. This has helped to produce the well known "lock step" in scheduling which is so counter-productive. The dimension of time as a variable, applied to all areas of the curricula, becomes a key element in the scheduling of a school program.

DAYS

	M	T	W	R	F
1	1	2	3	4	5
2	6	7	8	9	10
3	11	12	13	14	15
4	16	17	18	19	20
5	21	22	23	24	25
6	26	27	28	29	30
7	31	32	33	34	35

(PERIODS)

Figure 1-1
Traditional Schedule—
Seven Periods, Five Days

A number of attempts have been made at accommodating curriculum needs through the time variable even in the traditional schedule. For example, schools have doubled the time period one day a week in science courses to provide for lab work. Other courses in the curriculum receiving such favored treatment have usually been speciality or vocational courses, such as secretarial practice or graphics. However, this doubling of the periods often provides more time than is necessary. Furthermore, you can provide this "luxury" for only a few courses in the curriculum because it tends to become a bottleneck in a traditional schedule. Creating double periods of time in selective courses in the traditional schedule can cause serious constrictions in the scheduling of other courses. This is one of the reasons for looking seriously at alternate systems of scheduling.

The need for variable time blocks in the school schedule is based on the fact that many courses are taught in a school curriculum. These courses have different objectives, depending on the learning requirements. For example, data processing is obviously a course which needs extensive time periods on some days when machine boards are being prepared and run on the EDP equipment. A much shorter period of time, however, would suffice on another day when the activity involves a demonstration, lecture, or film.

This can be further and more dramatically illustrated by an anecdotal story of a foods class which took place in the Home Economics Department at Norwich Senior High School. At that time Norwich was using a traditional schedule which met for a 47-minute period each day. The teacher and students used Monday to plan a full course dinner—the quantity of food to be purchased and the division of labor involved in preparing the meal. Tuesday the food was prepared for cooking. Wednesday they began to cook, but because of the shortness of the period and the necessity of cleaning and putting away all pots, pans, and cooking utensils before the next class came, the food had to be put back in the freezer. Cooking was resumed and completed on Thursday. Fortunately the students were able to leave their other classes early on Friday and set the tables, reheat and eat the food thereby completing the activity.

Witness what happens to that old stalwart, physical education, when we apply some rationale to the course curriculum with use of time as a variable (Figure 1-2). At Norwich it was estimated that it took about 10 to 15 minutes to get the students dressed in their gym suits and out on the floor, ready for activity. Another 10 to 15 minutes was needed to return to the locker rooms, shower, dress, and get ready for the next class. This means that 25 to 30 minutes per day out of a 47-minute time period were spent on unproductive, repetitious acts. This left only 22 minutes for activity. Assuming the instructor wants 10 minutes to demonstrate or teach a new skill, this leaves only 12 minutes for reinforcement activity by the students. Naturally, the instructional time could be omitted, leaving students a full 22 minutes of "play," but no doubt this approach would be most unsatisfactory in many schools.

There is sure to be someone quick to point out that the aforementioned courses are speciality courses and that the argument used here would not be valid when discussing the "core" subjects such as math, language, English and social studies. But the fact is that there is a growing body of knowledge which tells us that time accommodations must be made in each course to fit the curriculum trends in the respective area. For example, it is known that intensive drills in speaking a foreign language quickly engender a mental fatigue. Perhaps 10 to 15 minutes is the optimum time for a student to do well. Thereafter, his learning curve falls off sharply. Perhaps a short meeting on the days intensive drills are held would suffice and the student could leave for still another experience. (See Figure 1-3.)

These are cases where the curriculum just does not fit the arbitrary time restrictions of a constant time slot. The list of examples which demonstrate that courses in a school program have been forced into a single time mold, thereby making the program the slave of time rather than its master, is as long as the number of courses offered in the program.

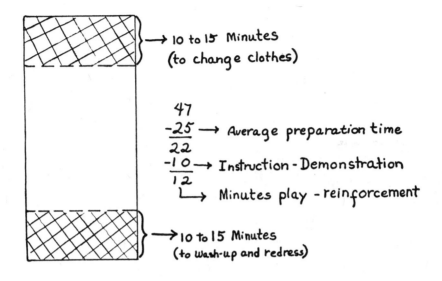

10 to 15 Minutes
(to change clothes)

47
−25 → Average preparation time
22
−10 → Instruction - Demonstration
12
↳ Minutes play - reinforcement

10 to 15 Minutes
(to wash-up and redress)

Physical Education Class
(traditional 45 minute block)

Figure 1-2
Physical Education Class—
Traditional 45-Minute Block

The Mod

The foregoing discussion should make it clear that any time unit used in a traditional schedule, whether it be 40, 45 or 50 minutes or any other specified time unit, is an inappropriate concept when applied to school programs. What is needed is a schedule that allows you to build a combination of time blocks to meet the different curriculum requirements of *each* course in the school program, with enough flexibility to vary the time from day to day depending on the activity.

This is done in a Flexible Modular Schedule through the use of a simple gimmick: the creation of a small block or module of time—say 15 minutes. Perhaps no class or group would meet for only 15 minutes but, by combining two such units, you can achieve a 30-minute meeting. By combining three of these 15-minute units, you can have a class meet on a given occasion for 45 minutes. The progression increases, and you can put

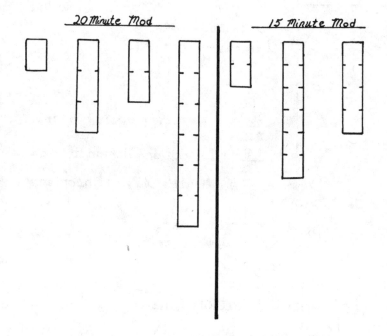

Figure 1-3
Time and Learning Activities

as many mods back to back, using them as building blocks, as is necessary to meet the requirements of the instructional mode. (See Figure 1-4.)

By changing the length of the basic time module, more or less flexibility can be gained. For example, a ten-minute module will allow you to build patterns of time around ten-minute intervals, permitting greater flexibility than you could achieve by using a longer time element. A ten-minute mod produces greater flexibility in that the variance of any block of time can be developed around ten-minute intervals (Figure 1-5). A 25-minute mod, conversely, produces less flexibility (Figure 1-6).

You can see that as the length of the mod increases, the variations possible in the length of the meeting period decrease. Most schools operate with a time mod ranging between ten and 25 minutes. The trend in the early days when modular scheduling was first being adopted was to use the shorter mods for greatest flexibility, but the experience of many schools is that a slightly longer mod is more desirable. Short mods tend to increase movement substantially with little overall gain. The tendency has been to use modules about 20 minutes in length.

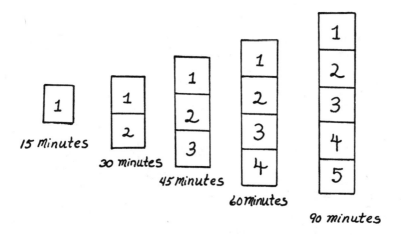

Figure 1-4
Mod Building Blocks

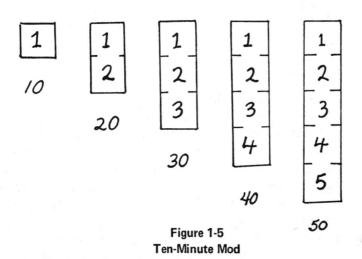

Figure 1-5
Ten-Minute Mod

In making the final determination, consideration will have to be given to a wide variety of factors including:

1. Past practice and length of period
2. Faculty attitude and acceptance of student movement between classes

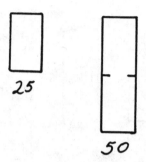

Figure 1-6
25-Minute Mod

3. Responsibility of a given student body
4. Length of school day
5. Degree of flexibility required (and desired) to accommodate program
6. Faculty acceptance of FMS philosophy

To be sure, there is no "right" length of mod. This can only be determined by consideration of all of the above factors—plus experience. One school that was visited has not used the same mod length two consecutive years for the five years that they have been in the program.

With the creation of the mod we have achieved the first step in our planned program to increase the school staff's ability to deal with the important curricular element of variable time blocks. Not only can they now design varying time requirements for a course but also they can alter them from day to day. That is, they can arrange to have the time configuration designed so that on a given day the course design may have one mod, two mods, three mods or more, or no mods at all—whatever amount is determined to be appropriate. This is important because in most cases the nature of the curriculum in a subject area will vary from day to day. On lab days in science much more time is required than on lecture days. When intensive language drills are being given in French, a student's learning curve drops sharply. On other days a planned cultural lesson might call for a more extended period of time. The illustration in Figure 1-7 demonstrates the flexibility you can achieve.

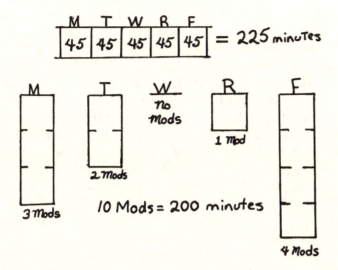

Figure 1-7
Comparison of Traditional
45-Minute Period with the Same
Course Designed on a
20-Minute Mod System

One criticism that has been launched against the flexible schedule is that once the time sequence is determined it cannot be changed from week to week. This is true. Once the time block for a given day is determined it repeats itself for the length of the schedule—5, 10, 20, 40 weeks. The word "flexible" in the name of the schedule refers to the phenomonon of being able to produce variable time blocks and vary them from day to day. It does not mean complete flexibility to change them on demand. Nevertheless, for the first time teachers can play a deciding role in helping to determine the design of a course, using time as an independent variable which can work to assist the school instructional staff in designing program. No longer will time control curriculum.

Variable instructional patterns

A second objective for school administrators interested in implementing Flexible Modular Scheduling should be the attainment of providing for variable instructional patterns in the school. Lloyd J. Trump and Dorsey Baynham in *Focus on Change; Guide to Better Schools*[1] proposed that students should meet in large groups, small groups or for individualized

---

[1]*Focus on Change; Guide to Better Schools*, National Association of Secondary School Principals (Chicago: Rand McNally and Company, 1961).

instruction, depending on the nature of the learning activity to take place. The book pinpointed its criticism on the traditional meeting patterns as being no longer flexible enough to deal with the changing demands on students in school and the way they learn. The recommendations made by the authors have had a tremendous impact on the educational scene so that today the need for variable class groupings is fairly well accepted.

For years a rubric of public education has been that the basic number of children in each class must continue to be reduced, irrespective of the nature of the learning situation. A major drive by teacher organizations along these lines has been characterized as heralding educational advances. In fact, the real issue, as Baynham and Trump saw it, is the basic inefficiency and waste inherent in the manner in which classes meet in the traditional pattern. In the old type of schedule teachers meet with 25 to 28 students in a classroom. At the secondary level the usual state maximum guidelines of no more than five sections to be taught by a teacher is a rule of thumb.

The serious problem of repetitious activity in a schoolhouse can be dramatically illustrated by a simple example (Figure 1-8). An English teacher who teaches five sections of 11th grade classes and who wants to show a 50-minute feature film has to use the entire day to show the film to each of his classes. Using a 50-minute period as an example, the total investment in the teacher's time is 250 minutes or more than four hours. Regrouping all his students so that the film could be shown once to a large group for 50 minutes would save him 200 minutes of time to be used for other types of activity, such as working with individual student problems.

The English teacher showing a film is just one example. If we add to this the many wasted professional hours used to monitor tests, repeat lectures, proctor composition writing or other such activity, the loss of time in such repetitious assignment is frightening. It would be far better if teachers used this time to work directly with students in establishing the personal student-teacher relationships so necessary if effective learning is to take place. With professional salaries continually on the rise, the cost to the public in lost teaching time through inefficient and repetitious activity is enormous; the loss in potential student learning is catastrophic.

Large group instruction

The most obvious and basic reorganizational pattern is that of restructuring classes into a large group. Although there are valid reasons for putting students in large groups, including the showing of films, testing, outside speakers, composition writing and more formal lecturing, it is important that the teacher feel comfortable with this mode of instruction.

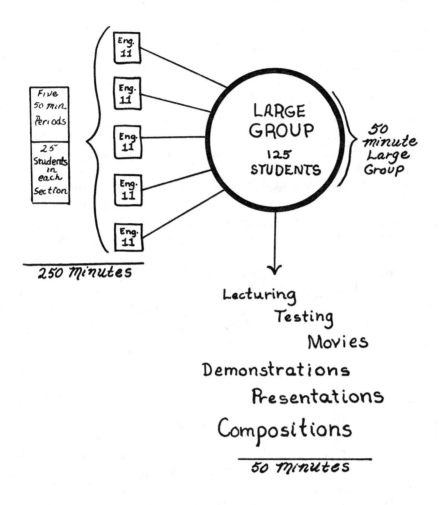

Figure 1-8
Regrouping

Facing 150 to 250 students in a large group presentation can, for one who is timid, be a threatening experience. For those who enjoy dealing with large groups and teach successfully in that mode it can be very rewarding.

Large group instruction tends to require more preparation and planning than other forms of teaching. It also requires a clear understanding of the objectives of this form of instruction and greater understanding of the use of support equipment, such as overheads. Initially Trump suggested that as much as 40 percent of the school instructional day will be spent in large groups. This seems to have been overly optimistic. Of all the different phases of instruction the large group is the most impersonal. For the most part the student is passive, an absorber of knowledge. Even under the best of circumstances, student involvement is at a minimum. These short-comings by no means negate the use of large group instruction as an important technique but the presenter should be cognizant of these weaknesses and plan around them.

In many cases large group instruction will be presented by a member of a teaching team, although a single teacher may also employ the technique. This is because the combining of a large number of students in the same course for more economical use of films and expensive equipment and for outside speakers makes this cooperative approach more feasible and economical. This combined grouping will have the benefit of utilizing the talents of the strongest member of the team for different subject matters. So much has been written about the advantages of team teaching that no further discussion about its merits is necessary. What is important is that the Flexible Modular Schedule will permit an unlimited amount of team teaching to take place with adequate teacher planning time built right into the schedule. At Norwich, the school moved from teaching teams and large group instruction in three courses to 12 teaching teams in two years.

Small group instruction

A second type of reorganization made possible through FMS is meeting students in small groups. Again, the literature is too wide in scope for the author to attempt to deal at length with the rationale of the importance of this type of instruction. It should be sufficient to say that *no school* can claim to do an adequate job of developing student communications skills, pupil interactions, individual and group leadership techniques, and group problem-solving approaches unless they make provisions for students to meet extensively in this phase of instruction.

Some of this is done in many schools through grouping within classrooms for certain activities, although secondary schools have been slow to adopt this basic elementary technique. It is often useful for the teacher to meet exclusively with small groups so that his undivided attention may be given to the needs of that particular group. Sometimes observing the manner in which a student performs in a small group setting can present greater insight into his needs an personality than an individual conference. In the latter, a student might be nervous or find it difficult to relate. However, in the peer group he should be able to demonstrate how he relates to his classmates; whether he is a leader or a follower, a cooperator or an obstructer, positive or negative, task-ori-ented or avoidance-prone. His group interests should be permitted to flourish and he should be able to demonstrate his communication skills. In short, the small group setting can allow the teacher to gain greater understanding and insights to guide the student with his learning needs.

Regular class

Meeting in a traditional class pattern is based only on history and logistics (most schools are designed with space cubicles to hold 25 to 30 students), since there are few curriculum justifications for meeting in groups of that size. The truth is that the regular class is too small for the practical showing of films, lectures, guest speakers, tests, composition writing, etc., and too large to be effective for good classroom discussion. A few students tend to monopolize these situations, and the range in abilities and interests, even in homogeneous groups, tends to be very wide. Continuing research into the problem of class grouping, such as that carried out by Columbia University's Institute of Administrative Research,[2] shows that although there is some difference in learning effectiveness related to class size it is teaching techniques that are the critical factor. Recognition of these principles is being incorporated into major breakthroughs in building design, such as those taking place in Little Falls High School, New York, which has movable walls and large, wide-open spaces with portable partitions to deal with the new concepts in school organization.

Certainly moving to a FMS will diminish the need and desirability of meeting groups of students in traditional groups of from 25 to 30. However, it will not eliminate it in all areas. The need to meet in this manner is dictated to a large extent by the habits and innovativeness of the school faculty or of any one department. At Norwich, for example, the 11th grade English faculty elected not to meet the students in regular classes at all. Instead, they restructured the program so that they met students only in small groups, large groups, or on an individual basis. Art electives met only once during the week for two mods in regular class. The rest of the time the students met in an open lab on an individual basis. The school health program was also organized to meet two mods in large groups and the rest in small groups. At the same time, some courses chose to meet in the traditional pattern of two mods each day. Again, the variations for the design of a course are open ended and dependent only on the innovativeness of the faculty.

Formal classroom time reduced

Fundamental to the transition and acceptance of a modular schedule is a phased decrease in formal structured classroom time. This has two

---

[2] "Identifying Quality in School Classrooms; Some Problems and Some Answers," *APSS Know-how*, Vol. 22, Jan. 1971.

"Classroom Variables That Predict School System Quality," *IAR Research Bulletin*, Vol. II, No. 1, Nov. 1970.

important bases; one is philosophical and the second practical. Today it is generally accepted that the need for face-to-face student-teacher classroom confrontation can be reduced because effective learning can and does take place outside the formal classroom setting. At the current rapid rate of the knowledge explosion our store of information doubles every 15 years. As a result, the emphasis in learning is shifting more to the research process, information retrieval and presentation of data than to the traditional teacher/classroom presentations. Reduced formal classroom time does not mean less learning. On the contrary, it means a greater emphasis on research-based work to be done during the student's out-of-class time. Some theorists have projected that formal class time will continue to be reduced until it assumes approximately 40 percent of a student's time, leaving the student 60 percent for other research, experiential school-sponsored projects or related activities. The practical reason for the reduction in class time is that it becomes extremely difficult to schedule a modular program unless the general rule of thumb is followed that students have approximately 35 percent unstructured time. Although this will vary considerably from student to student, the 65 percent structured classroom time is an average operational guideline. More unscheduled time tends to lead to control problems, especially if a strong backup program has not yet been developed. Less unstructured time can lead to scheduling problems because the scheduling can become too tight, causing excessive conflicts.

This savings can take place through a variety of approaches. When changing to a mod schedule and by shortening regular class time from that allotted in the previous traditional schedule, there will be a reduction in the time a pupil spends in class. At Norwich, the switch from a 47-minute traditional period to average class meetings of two mods or 40-minute periods in the mod schedule helped reduce class time. This initial savings of seven minutes six times a day resulted in 42 additional unscheduled minutes per day in the program. A second and more important decrease in structured time is realized through a planned decrease in class meetings. The decrease in time will vary depending on the course objectives and degree of sophistication of the teachers involved. This will be treated more fully at a later point; at this point it is sufficient to say that the reductions in class time should permit the creation of ample unscheduled time.

Course configurations

When we apply to the design of a course the two basic principles discussed so far, variable time length and variable meeting patterns, we come up with what is known as a course configuration. The course configuration is the product of the school's philosophy, course objectives, constraints such as room and teacher availability, and a multitude of other inputs. The configuration of a biology course (pictured in Figure 1-9) is a sample of a possible course configuration. It attempts to show how school personnel can begin to cash in on the many options offered by the Flexible Modular Schedule.

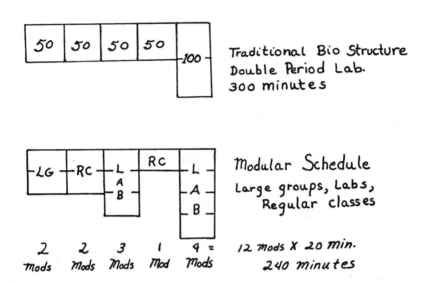

Figure 1-9
Traditional Bio Course Converted
to a Mod Schedule

3. Weighing Courses

In a traditional schedule, with few exceptions all courses meet five days per week for the same period of time and a set number of weeks. The only way in which time is used to control the relative importance of courses is by making them ten-week, half-year or full-year courses. There are some exceptions, such as schools offering physical education two or three times a week, or, as is sometimes the case in science or business courses, meeting a double period. However, the amount of flexibility in using time as a variable is obviously limited by the rigidity of the traditional time period.

Previously all courses were of the same basic design and were all offered for the same amount of time. For example, the courses shown in Figure 1-10 were offered in the Norwich High School program of studies.

We can question from even this small selection (actually NSHS had 100 courses, which ran on a regular five-day-a-week, single-period-per-day schedule), the justification for offering all these courses for exactly the same amount of time. Advanced French is a college preparatory subject

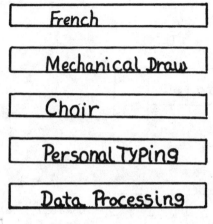

Figure 1-10
Courses Offered the Same Amount
of Time in a Traditional Schedule

requiring mastery of a number of complex skills, including talking, writing, translating a new language. A great deal of memorization is required and homework is almost always given. Not so with a course such as personal typing. Although there are definite skills to be learned (this is a non-vocational course) such as the keyboard, speed and accuracy, this course in the traditional schedule is granted exactly the same amount of time as French, advanced math and other courses requiring the learning of more sophisticated skills.

The reader may say that these are generalizations and that acquiring the skill of typing may require much more time for one student than learning French for another. This is true, and schools must take this into consideration in their programs. But when you are constructing a school schedule, certain generalizations must continue to prevail until such time as a school's schedule can be based entirely on individual needs. Although some schools are actually experimenting with "demand schedules," the cost and logistics problems have not yet made this approach feasible.

In FMS this can be easily overcome. First, careful consideration must be given to the objectives for each course and the way these relate to formal class time. Second, the modes of instruction to be used, whether large group, small group, lab or a great deal of independent study, will also play a role. Once these factors are determined you can construct a configuration based on the objectives of the program, using the element of time as an aid in determining that course's relative value to other courses in the curriculum.

Perhaps the most difficult task for the educator is to attempt to determine how much time should be given to a course. This represents a new area of professional decision-making with which few teachers have had experience. For the first time the educator can begin to tailor his course to the needs of the curriculum. The author once asked, when working with a college group designing course configurations, "How does it make you feel?" One student responded that it gave her a "tremendous sense of power." And indeed, the modular schedule gives power to the teacher for the first time to design a course school based on curriculum needs. Since the determination of the amount of time a course will require is central to the discussion of FMS, prior thought should be given to the parameters to be used. Specific guidelines must be developed when teachers are actually given the task of determining the course configurations. This is a key area and requires a lengthy discussion, which will take place in Chapter Three.

4. Greater Student Participation in the School Program

Most school programs are under-utilized by students. Witness the academic student who never sees the Industrial Arts Shop, the Mechanical Drawing Lab, the Art or Home Economics room. Or the vocational track student who attends a vocational center and is in his home school for only his required courses. How about the business student who is blocked out by double-period business labs, required courses and physical education? This description is the common theme in almost all traditionally scheduled schools. Although a FMS does not eliminate all of these problems, it addresses itself to dealing with some of the major obstacles to better school plant and program use by the students.

What are the problems defined? In today's concept of education, the needs of a student must be viewed more broadly than as being entirely academic or vocational. Decreasing time spent by workers on the job, rising incomes, sharply escalating costs of home services, etc., have resulted in two separate but equally important phenomena: one, a growing interest in the arts and other leisure-time activities with the time and money to pursue them; and two, the "do it yourself movement," ranging from household hobby activities to the more ambitious project of building one's own home. Provision must be made in the school program to allow students to enroll in courses which provide them with these necessary experiences if they are to be well-balanced and educated individuals. It is often impossible to fit into the schedule of the academic student in a traditional six- or seven-period day the non-academic but high interest courses necessary for a rounded education. At Norwich High School we found a number of students who had a schedule that completely blocked them in with academic courses, allowing them no more than three or four electives in their four years in high school. This meant that some students had no time to pursue interests in the non-academic curriculum areas, do independent research or even take a break during the school day.

A typical high school academic schedule may involve the following:

	9th	*10th*	*11th*	*12th*
1.	Language	Language	Language	Language
2.	Algebra	Geometry	Trig.	Calculus
3.	Gen. Science	Bio.	Chem.	Physics
4.	Soc. Studies	Soc. Studies	Soc. Studies	(Soc. Studies)
5.	English	English	English	English
6.	Phys. Ed.	Phys. Ed.	Phys. Ed.	Phys. Ed.
7.	Band/choir	Band/choir	Band/choir	Band/choir

Most schools run a large band, choir or orchestra program in which a high percentage of the students participate. As illustrated above, if a student takes either offering his program is filled in for his entire high school career. Some variation is possible for the inclusion of driver education or another course but there are very few exceptions until perhaps the senior year. *Most students have little spare time built into their schedules.*

We mentioned previously that there will be a considerable amount of unstructured time for students in a Flexible Modular Schedule. Although the objective is about 35 percent free time, students often have more than that. Students who have more than 35 percent free time can take the option of choosing an extra course in an elective area of interest to them. As a result of this new option the enrollment swells in such departmental areas such as business, home economics, industrial arts. This increased enrollment in elective areas is a stated objective of Flexible Modular Scheduling in that it meets the educational objective of permitting students to participate more fully in the total program rather than being limited to a specific group of courses. The longstanding complaints of students that they have no time to take interest courses because their schedule is too full will be a step further to being resolved with Flexible Modular Scheduling.

5. Unstructured Time

One major criticism launched against the public schools is that they do not allow the student to develop any responsibility for his own behavior while going through the schools. Decisions by teachers and administrators are continually being made for him every day, all day, providing him with little opportunity to assume initiative or make independent judgments. This paternalism of schools is often manifest in the inability of student government to display leadership, play an active role in school affairs or, indeed, even be able to determine their purpose or role. All the while this aspect of a young person's development is critical to his learning. Many students know how to use their time very well. Others have to be given the opportunity—through trial and error—to use their time more effectively. And there are some students, although usually a small percentage, who will never use their time well. It is these people teachers complain about, stating that they have too many study halls and get into trouble, or just waste their time away in class. Although teaching (or letting a student learn) how to use his time effectively is certainly a difficult area of responsibility, it is nonetheless a task that the school must assume.

Looking at the same problem from another perspective, it is well known that 50 percent of all students entering colleges are not capable of completing their courses. The factor most often identified as the cause of the student's failure to complete his advanced studies is not his academic incompetence but rather his inability to use his time effectively. The public schools are just not doing the job of developing in the student the proper social and emotional responsibility to cope with the more open and permissive college setting. This area of school concern is a new one, and it is just recently that more educators have begun to face the fact that besides the traditional domain of academic or vocational training and related "co-curricular" activities such as sports, theater, etc., the school must assume the responsibility for helping the individual become capable of using his free time constructively. A full discussion of the role that the program plays in relation to the use of students' and teachers' use of unstructured time is handled in Chapter Seven. Here it will be treated on a cursory manner in order to give the reader an overview of the basic program in a modular schedule.

There are a number of alternatives open to a student in a flexibly scheduled school during his unstructured time. These include:

Commons

This is a place where students can meet, take a break and socialize for short periods of time between classes. Often refreshments can be purchased.

Quiet study

An area can be set aside for quiet study. Unlike the old compulsory study halls where students were seated and attendance taken, going to this study hall is voluntary.

Instructional resource center

The updated library should be available to students all day. With the mod schedule, library usage usually grows considerably.

Laboratories

Several areas such as science, home economics, industrial arts and others may use their specialized classrooms as laboratories. These are open specified periods of time for students to come in for make-up work or to further pursue personal interests.

Resource centers

These are special departmental rooms used to augment the Instructional Resource Center. Faculty members man the individualized instructional phase of the program there. Often an aide covers the resource center, keeps track of special materials, gives make-up tests and performs clerical and housekeeping functions in the department.

A number of other options may exist, depending on the school's organization. Students tend to seek out help in guidance and administration much more often than in a traditional schedule. Mini-courses may be added to the curriculum for enrichment. Naturally, the more options a school can offer a student during his unstructured time the better it is. But in the final analysis a student must assume some responsibility for his own use of his free time. He must learn to initiate activities, seek out help, and use his time productively. No doubt different students have varying degrees of maturity and competency and each approaches the free time aspect with his own objectives. By beginning to deal with this facet of pupil behavior the school is entering a new realm of activity.

6. Increase Program Alternatives

With a Flexible Modular Schedule the school can concurrently operate other scheduling programs such as block scheduling, rotating scheduling, back-to-back scheduling and other options. Although these formats present constraints, the degree of flexibility in a mod schedule is much greater than the same program in a traditional school. The mod schedule further allows time for teaching teams to have planning sessions during the school day, a major advantage of FMS.

7. Reduce Monotony

The monotony of the traditional schedule with its lack of variation is well known both to students and to teachers. The stories about the "last period in the afternoon" or the "same thing day in day out" syndrome are part of the school lore. But this does not have to be. A flexible schedule allows the school to break the monotonous pattern of repetition by varying the instructional program. One of the most consistent bits of feedback from students about FMS is that they say school is definitely more interesting in FMS than in the traditional pattern.

Summary

In 1961 Trump and Baynham's important book, *Focus on Change, Guide to Better Schools*, was published. It spelled out what popularly became known as the Trump Plan. Flexible Modular Scheduling is the institutionalization of the Trump Plan in that it can schedule the reorganization of the school based on the principles of large group, small group and individualized instruction. There are seven main reasons for adopting this type of schedule: (1) to achieve variable time patterns; (2) to gain variable meeting patterns; (3) to weight courses; (4) to give students greater participation in the school program by allowing them to take additional electives; (5) to provide greater unstructured time for students; (6) to increase program alternatives and options for the school; and (7) to break the monotony of the traditional schedule. Each of these provides the school administrators with an increase in his options to implement more effective program for students. Team teaching is given as an example of a recognizable organization that can be readily designed into a flexible schedule with team planning time included in the school day.

2

The School Master Schedule

A master schedule is an educational blueprint, having the same relationship to the school program as an architect's drawings has to the construction of a new building. Through the vehicle of the master schedule, school planners must make basic decisions concerning the allocation of limited resources, the utilization of staff, length of time segments, five, six, or ten-day cycles, modes of instruction and course configurations. It may also be viewed as a statement of the philosophy of the school's administration personnel since they are ultimately responsible for its formation. In short, the master schedule reflects the extent of the thought and planning, theory and research, experience and expertise of its builders. This is best described by a reporter of the school scheduling scene who commented:

Indeed, the importance of the master schedule can hardly be exaggerated. It abstracts, in words and numbers, the essence of the school. For a given school year, it sets forth in precise detail who is going to do what for every period of every day in the week. Subjects, students, instructors, classrooms are all assigned. From the close study of a master schedule, a canny reader can learn much of a school: the programs it offers; the constraint or freedom that affects students' choice of courses; the school's position on the spectrum that runs from ultra-conservative or radical; its size, resources, shape—even its philosophy. In some schools, perhaps most schools, the schedule dominates the students and teachers it is presumably designed to serve. In a minority of schools, happily on the increase nowadays, the schedule reflects fresh efforts to enliven and individualize education.[1]

Traditional Scheduling

Perhaps 92 percent of all schedules reflect the traditional meeting pattern of classes in secondary schools, which arranges for six, seven, or eight class periods daily, each a standard number of minutes in duration, meeting five days a week for the length of the school year. The foundation and educational justification for such a schedule reside primarily in the Carnegie Unit method of awarding credits for time spent in class, a method which was instituted in order to bring some accounting uniformity between schools in different areas of the country. When first introduced, it was directed at dealing with the multitudinous course variations offered by independent school districts in the individual states. The objective of this attempt at categorizing and standardization was to make courses equivalent for college purposes and for students who were moving between schools from one area to another. In a sense it can be considered a national school accounting system.

Over the years schools have experimented with different schedules, using formats such as block schedules, floating periods, and rotating schedules. These devices attempt to deal with some of the basic problems inherent in the traditional schedule. In particular, these weaknesses include monotony, limited program involvement, over-scheduling and structuring of students, rigid meeting patterns unrelated to curriculum, and the general problem of arbitrary restrictions which the schedule forces on students. From a teacher's perspective, the traditional schedule blocked effective time for planning, meeting individually with students, grouping of students, making professional decisions about the use of time as a variable in determining the curriculum, and creatively involving the teacher in master schedule planning.

The Computer Impact

The computer began to make an impact as an administrative aid in the early 50's when IBM, GE and other computer companies entered the school scheduling field with programs to help beleaguered school administrators. Primarily the computers were programmed to load a traditional schedule developed by the school administration. The computer helped place students into the schedule. This is done by transposing the master

---

[1] Judy Murphy, "School Scheduling by Computer, The Story of GASP," Educational Facilities Laboratories (1964), p. 1.

schedule on punch cards and storing it into the machine. Then each student's course requests, also on cards, are run through and the students are "loaded" or scheduled. Students with conflicts are "rejected" and are later programmed by hand. The first to use these loading programs were the larger metropolitan high schools with enrollments in excess of 2,000 pupils. Today most high schools use some form of computer loading program to help them schedule. Although this is a great aid in helping administrators deal with the Herculean task of scheduling building, it did not deal with the basic question at hand—how to reorganize a school schedule to increase pupil-faculty options. Even with the aid of a computer, as long as the Carnegie Unit with its basic tenet of equal time in all courses and a "balanced" schedule were the prime objectives in a school, the schedule remained the key blocking element in any attempt to change.

The Breakthrough

> Every 50 to 55 minutes the comparative quiet of today's schools is shattered. A bell rings, students burst into corridors, tramp to other classrooms, doors shut, the bell rings again, and a new class period begins. The bell is no respecter of students' interest or teachers' plans. It cares little that equipment in some classes takes ten minutes to store or that presentations in others must be interrupted midway. Its sole function is to punctuate the day into six or seven exactly equal periods of time.[2]

These were the words of Trump and Baynham in *Focus on Change; Guide to Better Schools.* The book, authorized by the Commission on the Experimental Study of the Utilization of the Staff in the Secondary Schools, has made a lasting impact on the reorganization of the nation's schools. The authors laid the foundation for the major restructuring which is today taking place. The so-called Trump Plan is synonymous with the reordering of the public school along lines that are more economical, educationally productive and humane. And for the first time in an important manifesto, emphasis was given to the redesign of the school schedule to meet curricula needs based on identifiable criteria.

Generating the Master Schedule by Computer

> The reader would undoubtedly agree that building even the traditional schedule is complex, time consuming, frustrating, and often pure drudgery.[3]

---

[2]*Focus on Change*, p. 40.

[3]Donald Keys and Gardner Swenson, *Providing for Flexibility in Scheduling and Instruction*, Successful School Management Series, (Englewood Cliffs, N.J.: Prentice-Hall, Inc., 1966), p. 13.

The next step was to actually generate the construction of a master schedule by computer. This is the dream come true of all school schedulers. Few people who have never had to deal with the realities of building a school master schedule realize that it is really a difficult job. In fact, it is so time consuming that many schools rarely change their master schedules, or make only minor adjustments in them at the end of the school year, because of the magnitude of the operation. The more conscientious administrator each year tackles the rebuilding of the school master schedule, thereby reflecting changing student needs, goals, staffing, and resources. However, it is possible that—given the ever growing pressures on school building administrators—the percentage of schools that start from scratch each year is rather small.

Thus, the time was ripe when, at separate locations in the United States, experimental work was taking place on the concept of generating a school master schedule by computer. One of the centers was located at MIT where Robert Holtz began work on a system first designed to make the best use of that venerable institution's resources. The system was known as Generalized Academic Simulation Program, more appropriately shortened to the acronymn, GASP. In 1961, Mr. Holtz received an Educational Facilities Laboratory grant to develop the scheduling program, and by 1963 it had been refined enough to be offered to other institutions, particularly public schools. Initially, in 1963-64, four U.S. high schools experimented with GASP schedules. They were Wayland High School, Wayland, Massachusetts; Ridgewood High School, Norridge, Illinois; Cohasset High School, Cohasset, Massachusetts; and the Pascack Hills High School in Montvale, New Jersey.

Meanwhile, on the West Coast, another program was under development at Stanford University. In this case the financial aid came from the Ford Foundation. This program, the Stanford School Scheduling System, commonly known as the Quad-S or 4-S, was under the direction of Robert V. Oakford, Professor of Industrial Engineering and Dr. Dwight Allen,* Educational Administration.

> With the advent of electronic data-processing procedures, the high speed computers, the possibility of developing a flexible high school schedule, capable of providing an atmosphere wherein educators can conceive of and implement educational alternatives to serve the educational needs of pupils, has become a reality. These machines have been used in a variety of complex industrial, governmental, and military applications. They mark a new industrial revolution—freeing men from mental labors more prodi-

---

*Dr. Allen, then an Associate Professor at Stanford, headed the program.

gious than the physical labors eliminated by the power revolutions of the past two centuries. As a school schedule becomes more varied to provide for new levels of individualization, the number of schedule alternatives increases geometrically; what is an odious task under current practice, without mechanical assistance becomes an impossible task. The magnitude is incredible—if an 80-period week is used for 1,800 students, it would take a computer capable of a million operations a second about twenty-five years to consider systematically all alternatives possible for a single schedule. The use of computers, however, demands a much more thorough analysis of the problems and decisions involved than has been necessary under more straightforward manual systems of scheduling.[4]

The five original schools involved in the 4-S scheduling experiment included John Marshall High School in Portland, Oregon; Lincoln High School, Stockton, California; Overfelt High School, East San Jose, California; Homestead High School, Cupertino, California; and Virgin Valley High School in Virgin Valley, Nevada.

At Marshall High School Dr. Gaynor Petrequin, Principal, worked with his staff during the spring of 1962-63 on the foundations for their modular schedule. In his book, *Individualized Learning Through Modular Flexible Programming,* Dr. Petrequin relates:

Following several months of planning course structures, teacher assignments, and room utilization needs, basic input data were submitted to the Stanford Project. After four years of experimentation and the expenditure of considerable resources, Stanford produced the first computer-generated school program in August, 1963, for Marshall High School.[5]

The key figures in early schools to make the change expressed the point of view that the job could not have been done without the computer generating the schedule. Here, Dr. Petrequin, like many others, was swept away with the idea that the application of the computer was the only way that an FMS could be designed. Using his own words:

It would be physically impossible to manually prepare a master program with the complexity of the design used at Marshall or to assign the entire student body by hand to individual class sections; therefore, this continues to be performed at Stanford using the IBM 1790 computer. Although the computer is necessary to generate the master schedule and load students

[4]Robert Bush, Dwight Allen, Robert Oakford; "The Stanford School Scheduling System," School of Education and Department of Industrial Research (ERIC Document Ed. 028501, Stanford University), p. 6.

[5]Gaynor Petrequin, *Individualized Learning Through Modular Programming,* (New York: McGraw-Hill, Inc., 1968), p. 3.

into the schedule, it is necessary later to make some manual adjustments for certain individual students and to hand-schedule students new to the school.[6]

Dr. Petrequin, a pioneer in flexible scheduling, was to change his mind about computer scheduling some five years later.

Computer-Generated Schedules Go Commercial

As the computer programs passed from the experimental to the operation, the commercial interests took over. Today, the surviving program remains the Stanford School Scheduling System. This program has been absorbed by two companies, Westinghouse Learning Corporation with its home base in Iowa City, Iowa,[7] and Educational Coordinates, Inc., of California.[8] Among its more than 200 customers are a small number of elementary and middle schools. The majority of FMS schools are secondary.

GASP was also commercialized when the private consulting firm of Hewes, Holy and Willard was formed. However, this company was short lived and the program is now in the public domain. A number of school-operated computer centers use GASP for scheduling; it may also be purchased outright for a small sum. Unfortunately, it is extremely complex and there are few people qualified to work with it.

Administrator-Designed, Manually Constructed FMS

At first it was thought that only a computer could deal with the intricacies of secondary school scheduling. While the educational community was being captivated by the use of the computer and its application to schedule making, some independent schools withstood this early rush and began to experiment with administrator-designed, manually constructed Flexible Modular Schedules.

Limitations of Computer-Generated Schedules

Various techniques were developed, specifically aimed at dealing with the shortcomings which were becoming evident in the commercial computer programs. Besides developing new methods of hand scheduling, some schools used data-processing programs especially designed to help load students and print out class lists in a modular schedule.

---

[6]Petrequin, *Individualized Learning Through Modular Programming*, p. 7.

[7]Westinghouse Learning Corporation, P.O. Box 30, Iowa City, Iowa, 52240. Also, 100 Park Avenue, New York, N.Y. 10017.

[8]Educational Coordinates, Inc., 432 South Pastoria Avenue, Sunnyvale, California 94086.

The major drawbacks to computer scheduling programs experienced by many schools include:

Cost

A minimum charge using the Quad-S program is $4,600 for a school of 1,000 students. Thereafter, the fee goes up on a sliding scale.[9]

Large numbers of conflicts

The computer will not schedule students with any conflicts. Sixty to seventy percent conflicts is not unusual. These must be resolved after the last computer run—often in the middle of August.

Problems of restrictions

Restrictions in scheduling limit the computer's ability to generate a schedule. Since restrictions in a computer program are "either-or" propositions, a large number of options for the scheduler are eliminated.

Teacher program

It is difficult to distribute teacher schedules in early May or June with a computer-run program. Union or teacher representative groups might dictate that concrete schedules are completed before these late dates. Moreover, it might be expedient for planning purposes to distribute completed teacher schedules as early as possible.

Significant errors

A significant scheduling error or omission can be disastrous in a computer-prepared schedule. We have all heard of the school that didn't open its regular session on time because of a scheduling "failure." [10]

Decreased Flexibility

Building a schedule must be considered a master arrangement of compromise. It is the interrelationship of literally thousands of computations and permutations in class scheduling, the allocation of human and fixed resources and a major political document for the school community. Although it is sometimes suggested that moving to a computer will neutralize these elements, it may also move a venerable senior faculty member to five different rooms on three different floors. The point is that the computer programs significantly decrease the scheduling team's ability to work out many situations.

---

[9] A copy of the Westinghouse Learning Corporation Scheduling Contract can be found in the Appendix.

[10] Montclair, New Jersey, is one (1969).

Student program decisions

Snap decisions about student programming and arbitrary course assignments are often forced on a school when the computer-generated schedule arrives back at the school. As mentioned before, the late arrival of the completed schedule (with many conflicts) may lead the guidance staff to move to a crash program of student placement. It is difficult to individualize schedules only three weeks before school opens.

Backtracking

When a section is filled and a new student (perhaps his name begins with a "Z") needs to enter it or has conflicts with other key courses, the computer cannot backtrack to see if another student already scheduled can be taken out, placed in another section, and scheduled fully. This would create a space for the "Z" student and allow him a full program. The inability of any computer program to backtrack, whether generating a master schedule or just loading, presents a limitation.

Because of the above-mentioned factors, a number of schools still interested in the implementation of the Trump Plan and FMS moved to develop the administrator-designed, manually constructed master schedule. A number of other schools that had been involved in the early pioneering of the computer-generated schedules[11] also made the move to the manually constructed schedule.

Advantages of Hand Scheduling

The reason for identifying these problems is to illustrate that as more and more schools move to FMS, school personnel should be aware that there are alternate means of scheduling that can meet their objectives, other than the computer-generated schedule. Indeed, the administrator-designed hand-scheduling technique has demonstrated its competitiveness, utility and advantages over computer schedules.

After studying a number of separate situations and visiting schools from Florida to California, the Norwich leadership chose to schedule its school by hand. The reasons for this are outlined below:

1. A major factor was *timing*. By going the hand-scheduling route we were able to give each teacher a copy of his next year's schedule by the end of June. This factor weighed heavily in our program since faculty put a particular emphasis on it.
2. *Conflicts* can be worked out with the students individually during

---

[11]Of the four schools originally using the 4-S program, only one school, Lincoln High School, Stockton, California, still uses the computer-generated schedule.

the summer. Course alternates could also be made as a student was scheduled. Because of the high degree of incidence of some form of conflict in FMS (many schools report up to 40 or 50 percent during the scheduling process), a great deal of individual student programming must be done. A conflict can be an irresolvable, head-on collision between two courses, or just a single mod overlap on a certain day. Since many students take a sixth and even a seventh course, increased conflicts do result.

3. Subjects with poor course design in relation to the rest of the schedule can be spotted early and *adjustments* can be made. Teachers can be notified during summer months of the necessary changes in plenty of time before school opens.

4. Schedulers can *backtrack* and reschedule students into other sections when necessary. This cannot be done by a computer.

5. Much of school decision-making is based on precedence, personality (of the staff) and pragmatic *compromises*. In a computer-generated schedule the rules are "either-or," and it is extremely difficult to program such qualifying concepts as "under certain circumstances." This is especially a problem when there is a scarcity of resources such as classrooms, teachers, resource centers, duty schedules, etc., which make necessary continuous adjustments.

6. *Cost* is certainly a factor. Hand scheduling allows you a considerable savings in dollar outlay over a commercially prepared computer-generated schedule.

It was felt that with the aforementioned factors taken into consideration, Norwich could do a better and less expensive job by hand scheduling than by computer. This proved to be absolutely correct.

Flexible Scheduling in Rural, Suburban and Urban Schools

One of the interesting features of the growth and acceptance of Flexible Modular Scheduling in the secondary schools is that no category of school, rural, suburban or urban, is excluded. Indeed, the major success stories in the field seem to be spread among the three. When the first trial runs were made back in 1963, the experimenters aimed at establishing the program in each of the three categories of schools. John Marshall High School, a 2000-student inner-city high school, has been in the program since its inception. John Dewey High School in New York City is a more recent convert to the program. A large urban high school in California with a predominately Spanish-speaking population and only two percent going on to higher education was successfully scheduling FMS.

Further, a host of suburban and rural schools, of all sizes from 3,000 to 150 students, have adopted the schedule, some operating on FMS for as long as ten years. In addition, there is no clear pattern among the schools of the method used in implementing administrator-designed or computer-generated scheduling, nor is the schedule limited to just a high school. Elementary schools, middle and junior high schools and junior-senior high schools are also using FMS.

The schedule explained in this book, employed at Norwich Senior High School, Norwich, New York, a rural school of 800 students, grades 10 through 12, was based on techniques used in three other schools: a large urban public high school, a medium-sized urban parochial school and a large suburban high school. It is the experience of the author that the format outlined in this book may be used in any school setting, large or small, rural, urban, or suburban.

Summary

This past decade has seen the beginnings of a revolution in school scheduling. First the computer was used simply to load students into traditional schedules. When Baynham and Trump wrote *Focus on Change; Guide to Better Schools,* the way was open for a basic reorganization of the schools. The book furnished the impetus for a major breakthrough in the scheduling of schools, the computer-generated schedule. Called Flexible Modular Scheduling, this is today an important method of scheduling schools that have adopted the Trump Plan. At the same time, other schools found major weaknesses in the computer-generated schedules and began to use a technique known as the administrator-designed hand schedule. This practice has had wide acceptance and success. Its patrons include a number of schools that previously were on computer-generated schedules. Advantages to the administrator-designed schedule include a cost advantage, greater control over conflicts, better individualization of a student's scheduling, greater flexibility in dealing with scheduling variables and an important advantage in timing.

There does not seem to be any pattern or type of school, rural, suburban or urban, adopting FMS. The format of hand scheduling outlined in this book was used in a rural school but modified from systems used in other, larger schools. The system may be adapted to any setting.

Preparing to Build the Master Schedule

DESIGNING THE COURSE CONFIGURATION

In this chapter we will begin the actual work of determining the design of the configurations for courses in the school curriculum and tackle some of the many variables that affect their organization. The reader should be cognizant of the fact that it is the development of the course configuration that has the most significance for the learning program. How a teacher meets his students, the frequency and length of time they are together and the patterns in which they meet will have a marked impact on the overall school program. The faculty can now take advantage of the opportunity to break the lockstep of traditional school schedules and use time as a manipulative factor to be apportioned, at the discretion of the teacher, for legitimate learning ends. It is the teachers' understanding and acceptance of the advantages of the modular schedule and their ability to capitalize on the increased options in a Flexible Modular Schedule that will determine the extent of innovation and re-direction of the learning program. Earlier chapters dealt with the rationale for the schedule. Later chapters will deal with the technicalities of scheduling and the evaluation of the program, which determine whether it is all worthwhile. This chapter will focus on the essentials of designing course configurations in the modular schedule.

The Length of a Mod

At the center of any discussion of a flexible schedule should be a complete understanding of the mod itself and what determines its length in time. Earlier the mod was defined as a unit of time shorter than a traditional class period which can be used in combinations with other mods to allow for variable time patterns. A single mod may or may not be used for a separately scheduled learning situation such as a regular class or small group. This will depend on the length of mod used by the school, or on the department's philosophy. Remember, the shorter the mod the greater the flexibility in time patterns open to the school. Short mods, besides increasing the frequency of student movement, also curtail the option of a department to use a single mod. A ten-minute mod, for example, by itself is not considered an effective meeting time.

In establishing the length of the mod the school administration should bear in mind that historical considerations often play a role. If the class period in a traditional schedule previously was 45 minutes long, the choice of a 20-minute mod might be difficult for staff to work with. Two mods would give 36 minutes of teaching time and three mods would be 56 minutes. The first choice would leave a time span considerable shorter than most teachers are used to working with, while the second alternative might be longer than desirable.

The final determination of the length of a mod should involve faculty input. The school administrator would make a mistake if he forces a faculty to radically change their entire "time" reference. There are a number of exponents of Flexible Modular Scheduling who would use the schedule to coerce teachers to change their teaching techniques and methodologies. This approach is entirely unrealistic and actually produces negative attitudes. It would be far better to institute a good in-service program for faculty directed towards those ends rather than expect to arbitrarily impose a structure that will magically change the pedagogical process. The demands that will be made on teachers as a result of the reorganization of the schools through the institution of FMS will in themselves result in pressures on the faculty to make it work well. These should take primary consideration. Therefore, it is suggested that the school administration offer the faculty an opportunity to make the mod length meet their instructional needs, balancing both the school's historical factors and the demands for change.

The length of the module at Norwich Senior High School was 22 minutes. This module, worked out and agreed upon by the Department Chairmen's Committee, represented a true compromise between those who wanted a total departure from the familiar and accustomed time patterns and those who wanted no change at all. At Norwich the previous time period, before moving to a mod schedule, was 47 minutes. Adopting a 22-minute mod[1] reduced a two-mod meeting for a class to 40 minutes (22 x 2 = 44 - 4 = 40). Forty minutes was also estimated to be a workable period for large groups and small groups. Some of the faculty wanted to experiment with single mod classes and although 18 minutes (22 - 4 = 18) of learning time was considered short, it was felt to be workable in several areas including language (small group), and mechanical drawing (large group). Another advantage to the 22-minute mod was that classes that were scheduled for three mods, such as labs and some large groups, found the combination of mods in time appropriate to that curriculum. Teachers who have had a number of years' experience working with materials designed around a 47-minute time period could easily modify them and adjust the lesson a few minutes either way. In this way the program was modified along evolutionary lines rather than through an abrupt change.

Naturally no segment of time will meet all a school's requirements; each school will have to investigate its own set of unique and discreet variables to determine the appropriate length of mod to be employed.

Day Cycles

At this point a new scheduling concept can be introduced that may be especially helpful to school administrators and faculties looking to increase options in their school program. This is the value of *day cycles* as opposed to the current *weekly cycles* on which schools traditionally operate. There does not seem to be an answer as to who first introduced the idea in the field of education, but the Nova School in Florida apparently was one of the first to introduce it into their school organization.

A day cycle, in its simplest terms, is another method of gaining more flexibility and options through the manipulation of time patterns in the organization of a school. Whereas the modular concept refers to the vertical patterns of time blocks, the day cycle pertains to the horizontal structure of the days. In a traditional pattern the school days are coincident with the days of the week. Certain classes are held five days a week, Monday through Friday; some are held three days a week, Mondays,

---

[1]It should be pointed out that in a modular schedule passing time is taken from the last mod of a meeting pattern on any given day. If a school is working with a 10-minute mod and the school passing time has been set at four minutes, then a two-mod class in a program that has ten-minute mods will meet for 16 minutes (2 x 10 = 20 - 4 = 16). If the mod is 20 minutes in length, a two-mod class will meet for 36 minutes (2 x 20 = 40 - 4 = 36). Thus, the reader can quickly see that a one-mod class in a school using ten-minute mods is not very feasible.

Wednesdays, and Fridays; and in some schools a course might be offered twice or even just once a week. In a day cycle the Monday-through-Friday base is dropped and the days are given numbers or letters, such as 1-6 or 1-10 (depending on the number of days in the cycle), or A-F days, etc. Usually the object is to achieve an even number of days in the cycle, although there are some exceptions. This is how it works:

TRADITIONAL
WEEKLY   M T W R F / M T W R F / M T W . . .
CYCLE

6 (EVEN
NUMBER) DAY   A B C D E   F /A B C D   X E F
CYCLE

X–HOLIDAY

The fact that the cycle is one day longer does not mean that a student goes to school six days a week. What it does mean is that the day on which school opens, whether Monday or any other, is called "A" day. The second day is "B" day. Each day of the week takes on a new day schedule name until the day cycle is complete; then it repeats itself. Holidays, emergency school closings, etc., do not result in any change; the day cycle simply continues, carrying over the day the school is closed and continuing uninterrupted in sequence.

The obvious question to be asked is why should a school go on a day schedule? There are two primary reasons for this type of scheduling. One is that by going to an even number of days the school administrator gains greater balance in scheduling with a concurrent increase in building and facility utilization. For example, most schools schedule physical education three days per week. If one section is scheduled Monday, Wednesday and Friday, the scheduler is left with the task of scheduling the second section on the opposing two days with a third class in a different period on another day, or—as so many schools do—scheduling one class three days a week one semester and two days a week the second semester. By going to an even day cycle, two physical education sections, 1 and 2, can now be dovetailed, offering the maximum use of the gym station along with helping to balance student distribution.

Per. 1	PE 1	PE 2	PE 1	PE 2	PE 1
Per. 2					PE 2

Traditional Schedule—Two Phys. Ed. Sections

A	B	C	D	E	F
PE 1	PE 2	PE 1	PE 2	PE 1	PE 2

Six Day Cycle—Two Phys. Ed. Sections

A second reason for adopting a day cycle schedule is particularly relevant to the Flexible Modular Program. In a mod schedule many courses offer large group instruction at least once in a cycle. Large groups often serve the function of kicking off a new unit by a key lecture or outside speaker, showing a movie, or a wrap-up test. If the large group is missed, it can be a real impediment to the flow of the course content. In a traditional schedule this does not pose a problem because the teacher more than likely sees his students everyday. But in a mod schedule the teacher or team might not see all the students again for four or five days. The elimination from the school calendar of several Mondays (by new Federal legislation), emergency school closings, bomb threats, bad weather and other factors, all influence the learning program. This is a situation in which the modular schedule is especially vulnerable. In going to a letter (or number) day cycle, the school is able to deal with lost time so that there is no disruption to the learning program.

A	B̸	B	C	D	E	F	A	B	C̸	C	D	E DAY CYCLE
M	T̸	W	R	F	M	T	W	R	F̸	M	T	W WEEK CYCLE

Thus the labs, large groups, and all other activities scheduled for Tuesday, "B" day, are now shifted one day and Wednesday becomes "B" day. The teacher who had prepared to show a key movie can show it to the large group without any interruption. A minor revision of the entire school calendar to reflect the adjustment is made.

A third major advantage of the day cycle is that it offers teachers greater flexibility in designing their course configuration. A faculty may decide to work on a longer cycle than five days so that they may better space out certain phases of their course. Any number of days may be selected—2, 4, 6, 8, 9, 10, 12 (the upper limit is usually 12). Faculty members might select an eight-day cycle because they feel that having one large group every week (weekly cycle) is not enough, but having two such large groups is too much. Extending the number of days in the cycle to eight allows the more acceptable option of having two large groups per cycle. Naturally the same type of thinking could apply to small groups, labs, or any other mode of instruction.

A fourth and last major advantage is that the day cycle helps to break up the monotony of each day being exactly like the rest. It also assists in breaking up repetitive meeting patterns. Now everyone at school gets a turn at the Monday morning and Friday afternoon sessions.

As with all such changes there are always some drawbacks. If, for example, you lose too many days in the calendar, this will affect advance film orders that had been set months ago. It would also affect outside speakers engaged well in advance for large group presentations, since a change in the calendar will shift other large groups to a new week day. One other problem, which will be dealt with later on in Chapter Seven, should be mentioned here. As a result of moving to a day schedule, some students will be confused on any given day and will miss a class, or go to the wrong class on the wrong day. This type of misjudgment is not uncommon in a mod schedule, and adding the day-cycle concept tends to further confuse some students.

However, the day-cycle feature is very popular with both teachers and most students and, as long as they are aware of the shortcomings, it will prove to be a real advantage. (See Figure 3-1.)

Determining Course Time Requirements

Even before faculty begin the difficult task of deciding on the course configurations to be designed, parameters must be set by the administration. These guidelines will assist all faculty members to work within certain rules of the game. Two such parameters refer to the minimum and maximum amount of time that any one teacher or team may employ in designing their configuration. It is suggested, for example, that a guideline be established stating that no course may be designed for more time than that course used in the previous schedule. Since almost all courses run on a five-day-a-week basis this will affect all but a few specialty courses. The absence of such a rule would cause a number of individuals to demand *more* time than they previously had. Teachers who do this are not in tune with the philosophy and goals of Flexible Modular Scheduling, nor are they sensitive to the needs of other faculty who also must make demands on the student's time. Nevertheless, each faculty has one or more of these people on their staff, and it would be just as well to begin the scheduling process on firm ground rather than to have to argue later on the merits of each case. If, as a bona fide exception and because of some special or unique circumstance, the administration wants to increase the time of a course, it may of course negotiate this separately. Schools that

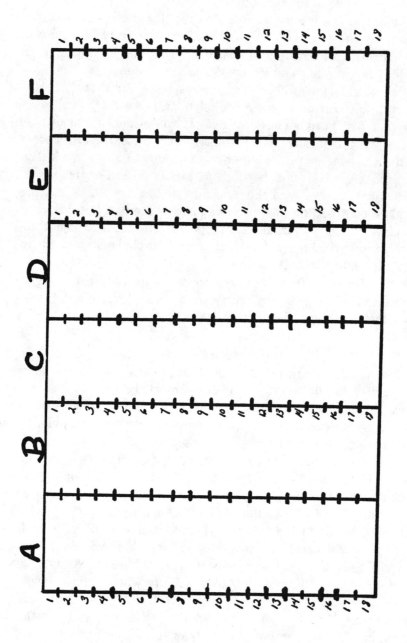

Figure 3-1
Six-Day Cycle, 18-Mod Day

have not enforced this guideline have often been boxed in with a schedule that is very tight, or have run into conflict between staff members. Faculty should be reminded that the idea is to reduce formal classroom presentations for greater independent study (IS) time for the student.

Setting Minimum Time Requirements

On the other end of the scale are the overly zealous enthusiasts who would reduce formal classroom time too much. These are the people who see students, once "turned free," as desiring knowledge in quantum amounts. Well, this would be utopian for anyone to expect and, to this writer's knowledge, it has yet to happen in any school. Certainly there are many individuals who would respond in unstructured situations very favorably and act in a model way. But it would be too much to expect all students to perform satisfactorily in a highly unstructured setting unless they have been trained for it in their earlier home or school experience. Thus, the amount of IS time designed into a course should be directly proportional to the free time activity which the teacher can meaningfully integrate in his program. A teacher must assume responsibility for a student's use of his unstructured time through the formation of resource-directed activities that require the student to use his free time to complete his class requirements. (This does not mean that everyone does exactly the same thing, e.g. in math, all students should complete problems 1 through 25 on page 108 of the text; prior to mod scheduling they had to do only 1 through 8.) Course materials such as Learning Activity Packages (LAPS), UNIPACS, and commercial individualized instructional material will give the program the necessary diversity and back-up activities for the proper student use of his unstructured time. In fact, schools contemplating Flexible Modular Scheduling would do well to give special emphasis to the development of an effective unstructured time program. Eventually the success or failure of the entire program will hinge on this feature.

It is interesting to note that there will exist a tendency for teachers to want to give more unstructured time to non-academic classes than to academic courses—even though everyone will readily admit that the students in these courses are the ones who are least able to handle the free time. This contradiction is explained in part by the fact that teachers are unanimous in their opinion that the slower students are more often bored by the classroom experience and less able to cope with the traditional structure. But if they are not in the classroom and they do not have meaningful out-of-class activities, what are they to do? This very important point must be dealt with in any school contemplating FMS. It is for this reason that a gradual approach to the question of IS time in the school is encouraged. Many schools have vocational school tie-ins, early release options, work-study programs or other programs at work. Others would do well to be cautious about excessively reducing student time in class until the faculty has completed the necessary curricular requirements for organizing an effective IS program.

At Norwich a course configuration guideline for minimum amount of time allowable for any given course was 65 percent of the previous year's schedule. This was a relative cut-off based on an estimated calculation that students with an additional 35 percent of free time would not be altogether unstructured or have an inordinate amount of free time. In general, this worked very well as a scheduling parameter and was a useful guide when working with the faculty in curriculum planning. (See Figure 3-2.)

The Appendix contains a course configuration packet used at Norwich in helping the staff design their courses. The packet includes a considerable amount of information germane to designing a course configuration. It includes a conversion table from a 47-minute period to a six-day, 22-minute modular cycle.

Selecting Modes of Instruction

Perhaps the most difficult task of the entire process is for the individual teacher or faculty team to select the modes of instruction to be used in the course to be offered. There is a growing body of literature that reviews the various modes of instruction, including large groups, labs and the regular classes, so that a reader who would like to delve more deeply into the comparative value of different meeting patterns has ample opportunity to do so. The problem in the development of configurations is that few teachers have had adequate training in the objectives of the various modes of instruction. Furthermore the objectives, methodologies, skills, and teaching techniques used vary widely between the modes. Since most teachers are experienced primarily in regular class instruction it is difficult for them to identify just what kinds and how much of the various modes should be employed.

The entire question of the choice of which modes of instruction to be used is very complex. Let me mention just a few of the factors to be considered: the nature of the course objectives; the ability of the teachers to differentiate between techniques; the question of whether or not the group is operating in a team; the major direction of the course; the school clientele being served; the commitment of a faculty to experiment; the physical facilities available; and many, many more. Often the first round of course configuration design represents some guesswork on the part of

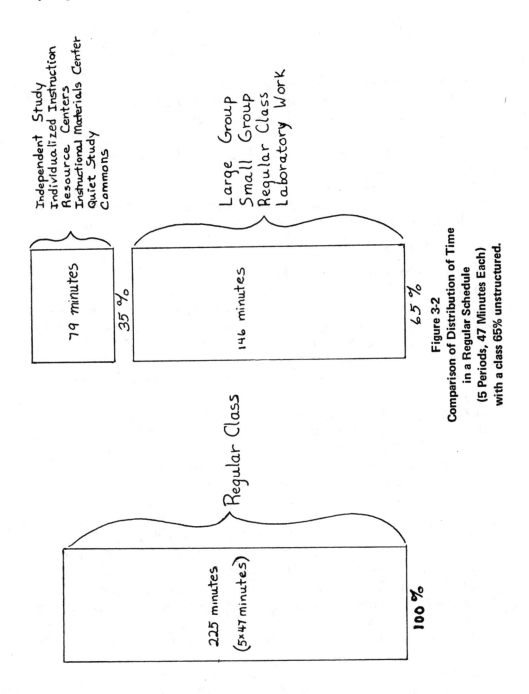

Independent Study
Individualized Instruction
Resource Centers
Instructional Materials Center
Quiet Study
Commons

79 minutes

35 %

Large Group
Small Group
Regular Class
Laboratory Work

146 minutes

65 %

Regular Class

225 minutes
(5×47 minutes)

100 %

Figure 3-2
**Comparison of Distribution of Time
in a Regular Schedule
(5 Periods, 47 Minutes Each)
with a class 65% unstructured.**

the teachers. Since most faculty have not previously worked with small or large groups they cannot make decisions based on experience but rather on what they feel they would like to do. After the first year of experience, however, there will be a refinement of the configuration; from there on course configurations will change as the teachers gain professional growth and the expertise in working with the different modes of instruction. Chapter One gives a brief overview of the modes that may be used. For further reference, Trump's book, *Focus on Change; Guide to Better Schools* (previously mentioned), gives a fairly detailed outline of the various modes of instruction. Currently there is a great deal more attention being shown to this area of concern, and material is being developed about the relative effectiveness of the various techniques. The reader can refer to the bibliography in the Appendix for other literature.

Restruction on Course Design

It would be well worthwhile for the school administration to establish some known restrictions and parameters within which the faculty will operate when designing the configurations. One of these should be the maximum number of consecutive mods any particular course may meet on a given day. For example, no faculty member should be allowed to request too many consecutive mods since it would disrupt the schedule and block too many other courses. What the actual parameters will be vary from school to school and also in accordance with the length of the mod. At Norwich, the maximum number of mods permissible consecutively was set at five which, with a 22-minute mod, is 106 minutes. However, no one requested this much time on a given day. The following year this parameter was reduced to four mods (84 minutes). It was interesting to note that courses which previously had a double period (94 minutes) in the regular schedule[2] willingly reduced their labs to three mods or 62 minutes.

Another major restriction on the course design is the fact that any course taught by more than one teacher—whether it is a team-taught course or not—must have the same configuration and time requirements. This is understandable since students transferring or changing their schedules would otherwise be confronted by an endless variety of meeting patterns. The process of asking each department to work together to determine some commonality in their course configurations makes for some interesting discussions and teacher amalgamations. Often people who teach the same course in the same department for years experience a

---

[2]Norwich, like many other schools, ran a number of Vocational and Industrial Arts courses as well as science labs with a double period.

new awakening when confronted with having to discuss such fundamental learning process considerations as teaming, modes of instruction, course time requirements, etc., with fellow faculty members.

Restrictions on course configurations may work both ways. That is, the faculty may impose certain restrictions on the school scheduling team. For example, a department or teacher drawing the course configuration may request that they meet a student in his small group only after he has first met in his large group session. Or the department may request that large group meetings have adequate set-up and break-down time, as might be necessary in a course requiring a great deal of demonstration material. Such a designation as "day independence" is also used. Day independence means that on no occasion may a class course meet in any mode more than once on the same day. For example, a course may frequently have a large group and small group meeting on the same day under a day independence guide. Day independence forces the scheduler to separate each phase and meeting time on different days.

Another restriction that can be placed on the scheduler is Exclusive Student Scheduling (ESS). This eliminates any cross-sectioning of students when there is more than one section operating in the course. Suppose there were six chemistry sections operating with one large group for everyone, a number of labs, regular classes, and many small groups. In a school with mod scheduling, a student would be able to attend any small group or lab he could be scheduled into even though the teacher might not be the one teaching the regular class or large group. Since each section has the same configuration and he is being tested in large groups, it is assumed that the course objectives are reasonably the same from section to section. Many times, however, and often for good reason, ESS is asked by a teacher, thereby putting a restriction on the scheduler. In that case each student assigned to his original teacher must take all that instructor's regular classes, labs or small groups.

Each school will have to work out its own scheduling restrictions; those outlined here are some, although by no means all, of the major ones. The list is as varied as the members of the teaching staff or the administrators of the schools.

FACULTY WORK SHEETS

Once the course configuration has been established by the individual teacher, team or department chairman, it must be communicated to the administration. In the Appendix there is a complete packet to guide a faculty through this process. Included in the packet are faculty work sheets which will be used to draw out the configuration.

The faculty work sheets illustrated in Figure 3-3 and Figure 3-4 depict the course configuration from the viewpoint of the student's schedule, not the teacher's. This means that if a course has a two-mod small group as a mode of instruction meeting once during the cycle, the small group will be drawn in only once on the configuration sheet, even though that faculty member will obviously have two small group sessions in his own schedule. The faculty work sheet should include all pertinent data to the scheduling of that course. Information concerning set-up time for large group instruction, team meetings, day independence, special requests, etc., should all be included on these sheets.

The work sheets when completed are turned in, by a set due date, to the administration, where they undergo a review.

SPECIAL REQUESTS

On occasion, special programs or special requests present unusual demands on the scheduling team. These special items are done in cooperation with administrative input and interaction so that they are no surprise. Usually they involve large groups or teams of teachers. An example would be the mixed English/social studies program at Norwich. This was a highly individualized non-academic track program, organized around field experiences, gaming, and resource-centered activities. The course met for four mods each day with four teachers all scheduled in a single block. One of the advantages of the modular schedule is that this type of block scheduling can take place for a particularly important curricular offering. Most schools take advantage of this feature in the flexible schedule by introducing such arrangements as block scheduling, back-to-back scheduling, floating mods or rotational features in the school organization. The variations can be quite extensive. Because of their scheduling demands these programs must be given special consideration by the administration.

FACULTY-ADMINISTRATION COMMUNICATIONS

Now begins one of the most productive aspects of the process of manually constructing a modular schedule. This is the give and take that occurs between the faculty and the administration when reviewing together the course configurations. As the administration reviews each course, questions will arise concerning the who's, why's and what-for's in course configuration requests. These are handled through extensive discussions and negotiations between faculty and administration. This communication is essential if the schedulers are to gain an understanding of the intent of the departmental requests. Later, when scheduling actually

WORK SHEET

Tentative Configuration
To Be Submitted For Each Course

Department _____ Course _____

Teacher(s) _____

	A	B	C	D	E	F
1						
2						
3						
4						
5						

A,B,C,D,E,F - Six Day Cycle
1,2,3,4,5   - Mods (Maximum is 5 successive mods for labs only)

Add Special Considerations

Team	_____
No. of Planning Mods	_____
Set-Up Time	_____
Others	_____

Figure 3-3
Faculty Work Sheets

WORK SHEET
Tentative Configuration
To Be Submitted For Each Course

Department __Science__   Course __Chemistry__

Teacher(s) __Joyce   and   Tulley__

	A	B	C	D	E	F
1	Large Group	Regular Class	↑	Large Group	↑	↑
2	all Students	↓	Lab	all Students	Small Group ↓	Lab
3						
4			↓			↓
5						

A,B,C,D,E,F -- Six Day Cycle
1,2,3,4,5 -- Mods (Maximum is 5 successive mods for labs only)

Add Special Considerations

Team
No. of Planning Mods __6 per cycle__
Set-Up Time   __one mod set-up and break-down before and after__
Others   __all small groups must follow large group. each large group.__

Figure 3-4
Science Course Request Sheet

begins, a number of compromises will continue to take place as an ongoing part of building a master schedule. Often adjustments must be made, and the better and more thorough the scheduling team's understanding of the course to be offered, the more closely they can adhere to the spirit and design of the course configurations request. The teachers involved will also gain insight through discussing their own work with the administration. New perspectives are presented and problems hashed over which perhaps were not thought of before. This interaction acts as a check and balance mechanism, keeping course configurations consistent with other scheduling demands and realities. It further helps weed out unworkable or difficult scheduling combinations and identifies certain potentially difficult configurations that will need special attention.

Administrative Review and Final Approval of Configurations

The last step is now ready to be taken before the actual construction of the master schedule. After the faculty-administration discussions have taken place and it is felt that there has been good communication, the final review process begins. The scheduling team, armed with a course configuration for each of the program offerings in the school, now begins its final review. Each course configuration is rechecked for accuracy and understanding. It is then initialed and laid aside and prepared for placement into the master schedule.

Summary

The first step in building the master schedule is to develop course configurations for each course in the school program. Several factors must be considered: the time restrictions that serve as parameters in the program and the modes of instruction to be used. Time restrictions are mutually imposing—those of the administration on the faculty and those of the faculty on the administration. Administrative restrictions are guidelines for the entire faculty; those of the faculty are specific to a course configuration and the way a teacher will meet his students.

A number of other techniques are used in developing a course configuration in a flexible modular schedule. Day cycles can be introduced; this adds a further option in creating scheduling flexibility.

Most important is the need for good faculty-administration understanding and communication. As the course configurations develop and later are scheduled, a number of adjustments and compromises will be necessary. Solid administrative understanding of well-developed faculty initiated course configurations will help in making a good master schedule.

Building the Master Schedule: Part I

THE SCHOOL SCHEDULING TEAM

With the rendering of the course configurations, the faculty has completed its major input into the scheduling process. Now the school scheduling team, usually comprised of the principal, assistant principal and guidance director, takes over. It is important that at least two of the three remain active throughout the entire process because, unlike the conventional schedule situation, there will have to be a great deal of give and take, adjustment and modification. No one man can analyze all the variables that will affect the construction of the master schedule. Two or three people who interact well together will be able to do a better job than a single scheduler. Some schools may have a full time scheduler or another staff member responsible for scheduling who would be a member of the team. Whatever the scheduling team's composition, at least one member should be charged with the authority to make adjustments or reasonable changes as the scheduling of courses progresses. Certainly major problem areas will need the involvement of those charged with the responsibility of the school curriculum, including the principal and teachers affected. Once the scheduling team has been identified the participants can begin their work.

MASTER SCHEDULE ROOM

It is important that a separate area, designated the scheduling room, be set aside in the school. This should not be used for any other purpose during the scheduling process because the basic tools of scheduling require considerable room. The orderly nature of the "clutter" cannot be disturbed without possible loss of important continuity from one scheduling session to the next. There should also be enough wall space for the faculty scheduling board and the room schedule board, and most importantly for the master schedule itself (Figure 4-1). In the event a school does not have an adequate scheduling "headquarters," the operation can be done by working out of loose-leaf books, but it is more time consuming for the schedulers to scan a set of loose-leaf scheduling sheets than a master schedule board.

Because of the pressures of the day, many school officials choose to do their actual scheduling at night. No special time is suggested by the author. Certainly the faculty conferences should take place during school hours because the personnel are there. The other times chosen for the work depend in large part on the staffing arrangements of the school, and the availability of the people involved and their inclination to work in the evening.

THE TOOLS OF SCHEDULING

When any journeyman embarks on a job to be done, the proper tools will help to aid him in the accomplishment of his task. This is true too for the scheduling team. The tools of scheduling include the following items:

1. Priority phase cards
2. Scheduling tags
3. Conflict matrix and course tally sheet
4. Faculty schedule board
5. Room schedule board
6. Master schedule board

A short explanation of each of the tools of scheduling should help prepare the school administrator for the next stage—the actual scheduling.

Priority Phase Cards

The first task of the scheduling team is to transfer the data received from the faculty from their course configuration sheets to special priority phase cards. (Figure 4-2). These are 3" x 5" or 5" x 8" cards which contain the necessary data for the scheduling team to begin determining the courses and the separate phases thereof that should receive priority when scheduling commences. Figure 4-2 shows how the cards present the information from the course configuration sheets (on the left) and a

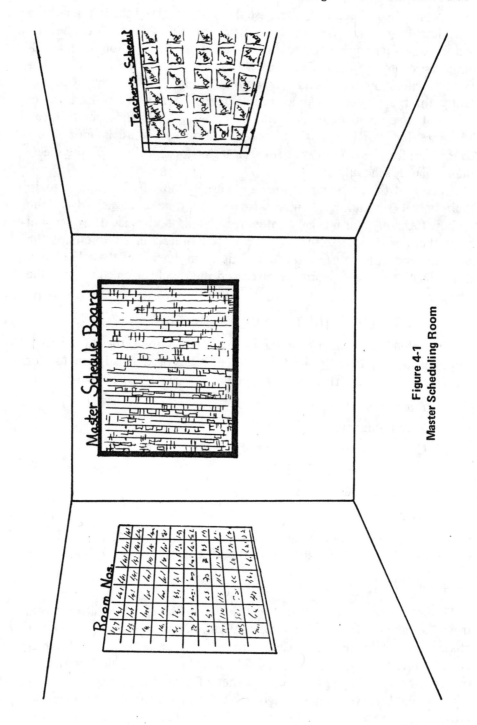

Figure 4-1
Master Scheduling Room

CODE	COURSE TITLE	MODE	MPC	MPM	SPS	STU	GR	PRIORITY

TEACHER   NO. SEC

SG SECTIONS ☐
LG SECTIONS ☐
RC SECTIONS ☐
LB SECTIONS ☐

1. SG____ M____ X

2. RC____ M____ X

3. LG____ M____ X

4. LB____ M____ X

Figure 4-2
Priority Phase Cards

breakdown of the information into modes of instruction, to be placed on separate priority cards, on the right.

Each priority card carries the following information:

1. The mode of instruction (L.G., R.C., S.G., LAB)

2. Number of meetings per cycle (MPC) (1X, 2X, 3X)

3. Number of mods per meeting (MPM)

4. Teacher(s) teaching the course

5. Other modes of instruction used in the same course

The reason for duplicating the information on each card is that after all the course configurations have been transferred to priority cards they will be separated (Figure 4-3). Having the data on each card allows the scheduler to review the entire course at any time without having to interrupt his scheduling to refer back to the original course configuration sheet.

SETTING SCHEDULING PRIORITIES

The next step is to begin the important process of ranking each phase of each course and assigning it a priority number. If there are 100 courses

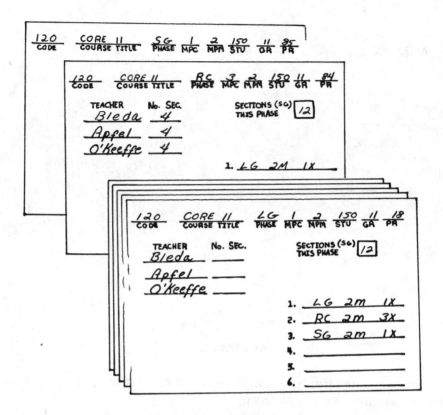

Figure 4-3
Priority Cards Separated

in the school program and if each course averages three modes of instruction, the number sequence in cards would range from priority card 1 to number 300. The number given each course and mode of instruction will be based on the same criteria that have always governed the scheduling of school courses. The determination of the priority is the reflection of several factors, including the school's philosophy, instructional objectives, learning priorities, student clientele, allocation of space and resources, and others. No two schools would rank all courses in the same relation to each other because of these differences and the author does not have any specific recommendations on course ranking, although there are guidelines to follow in the ranking of modes of instruction.

The entire objective of this operation is to rank in priority the courses and respective modes that will be scheduled on the master schedule board.

Stated simply, those courses that have the highest priority (lowest numbers) are scheduled first. The lower the number, the less prone the mode of the course is to conflict. As an illustration we can use the school band, because the band services a large block of students who cut across all grade lines in many schools. Since the band also includes many academic students who are usually fully scheduled, the large group mode of instruction in this course in many schools would receive a very high priority and is therefore scheduled early—perhaps even given priority number 1 or 2. To do otherwise might find the course being scheduled after many others and causing a considerable number of student conflicts. Few school administrators relish telling a parent their son has to make a choice between band and chemistry for the ensuing year. However, the band director may also have requested that he be able to meet small groups from the band, such as woodwinds, percussion, or brass. It is up to the scheduling team to determine whether these groups should receive a high, middle, or low priority. Some priority considerations are listed below for schools to review—but bear in mind that each school must make its own determinations:

1. Groups that are large and cut across multi-grades
2. Large group singletons
3. Large group doubletons
4. Blocked scheduled courses
5. Courses using specialized classrooms
6. Singleton courses, whatever mode
7. Doubleton courses
8. Tripleton courses, etc.
9. Labs
10. Regular classes
11. Small groups

Within the general priority patterns a more precise distinction of priorities should be established. This refers to such distinctions as grade level singletons, doubletons, teacher assignment, etc. (See Figure 4-4.) When this has been done the final result is a single deck of priority phase cards containing one card for each phase of each course offered and ranked in the order in which they will be scheduled in the master schedule (Figure 4-5).

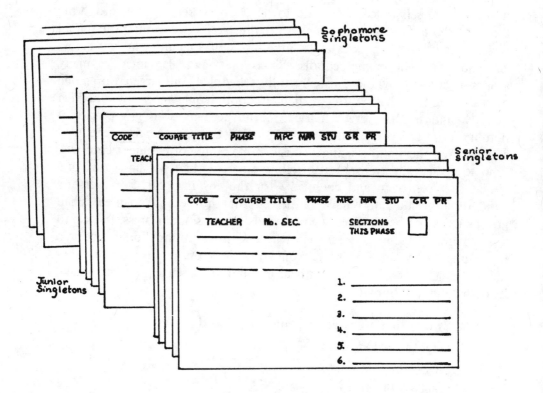

Figure 4-4
Priority Grouping

SCHEDULING TAGS

Scheduling tags are now made for each phase of each course and for the number of meetings and sections that the course will meet (Figure 4-6). If there are ten sections of English, each using three modes of instruction, 30 tags will have to be made. Tags should be colored for each grade level represented, with an additional color for courses that are fairly evenly distributed. Since many high school courses are somewhat mixed, the course receives a specific color designation only if the predominate number of students in that class are from the same grade. The information on that tag should include:

1. Abbreviated name of course

2. Section number

3. Number of students in the course by grade level

4. Mode of instruction

Figure 4-5
Phase Cards in Their Order of Priority

To insure that each course has the proper number of tags, the tags are clipped to the phase cards which are now in the priority deck. When this has been completed each phase card should now have a tag for every meeting, large group, regular class, lab, or small group which must be scheduled. When we begin the actual scheduling, each of these tags will be removed from the phase card, attached to a magnet and placed on the master schedule board. When all of the tags have been placed or accounted for on the board the master schedule will be complete.

Conflict Matrix and Course Tally Sheet

No schedule, conventional, modular or any other, should be designed without a conflict matrix. The matrix is simply a cross tabulation of student course requests which serves as a reference to the scheduler. It informs him how many students taking any one course are also taking another. For example, it is useful for the scheduler to know how many students taking intermediate algebra are also taking Spanish 2. If there are

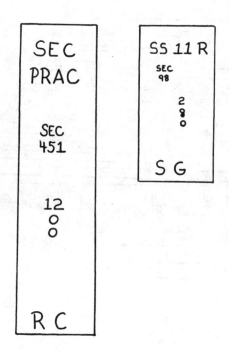

Figure 4-6
Scheduling Tags

no students taking both courses, he is free to schedule them simultaneously in the master schedule without having to worry about "conflicting" any students out of a course. If there are many students who have requested both intermediate algebra and Spanish 2 in their course requests, then it is obvious to the scheduling team that the two courses should be scheduled on separate periods or different days. If there are only one, two, or three students who would conflict, the schedulers will have to make a decision based on the relative importance of the courses, what year they are offered, and whether or not they are sequential. The value of the conflict matrix is that with it you reduce significantly the risk of increasing course conflicts.

Whenever possible, assignments of personnel should take place prior to the design of course structures so that the individual teachers may be involved. However, until the conflict matrix and course tally are run, staff assignments cannot be finalized. Once the tally is complete, staffing decisions must be adjusted to meet student needs. Often in larger schools this is done at the department level with the chairmen presiding. In any event, all the final assignments are reviewed by the principal for equity and maximization of use of personnel based on the data received from the tally sheets.

Running a conflict matrix for a school is a simple but important job done by electronic data processing. Any commercial computer center in the educational business can run a matrix. The initial data is gathered when the school counselor interviews and programs each student in the spring of the year. Each course selected by the student has a popular name and is also assigned a data-processing number. Thus the course appears on the sheet as 519 Spanish 2. (See Figure 4-7).

When the student course request sheets are finished they are turned over to the data-processing center. There a key punch operator takes a card for each student and key-punches in his name, identification number (right from the school census) and the data-processing numbers from each course request that he made (Figure 4-8).

The numbers are then tabulated and cross-referenced electronically. The resulting machine print-out indexes each course code number in the school curriculum and identifies the number of students who are taking any two courses. This is what is known as the conflict matrix (Figure 4-9).

Besides the conflict matrix the scheduling team receives other very important data, such as the course tallies from this run (Figure 4-10). The course tally gives us the number of students who have asked to take each course in the program. Perhaps the school administration had planned on five chemistry sections to service 120 students, only to receive the tally sheets back and discover that 175 students requested chemistry for next year. Decisions will have to be made with regard to the final number of students for whom the course is opened, the hiring of additional personnel, room space, and so on. Conversely, too low an enrollment might see the elimination of a section and the reassignment of personnel to other areas.

Faculty Schedule Board

The faculty chart uses the same format as the student schedule. One sheet is made up for each faculty member (Figure 4-11). As a course is scheduled on the board, the teacher's schedule is also filled in at the same time. This blocks him out and prevents a teacher-scheduling conflict. A careful watch must also be made to see that enough time is scheduled for the teacher's lunch and preparation time and for any other contractural arrangements that need to be taken into account.

1972 -- 1973
NORWICH SENIOR HIGH SCHOOL
Student Program Sheet

name _____
_____ hmrm ___ yr ___
Sex ___ COUNSELOR _____

mods _____
% struc _____

ENGLISH
110 Mess 10
115 Eng 10R
116 Bus Eng
120 Core 11
125 Eng 11R
130 Eng 12NR
135 Eng 12R
145 Grt Idea A
146 Grt Idea B
175 Cinema A
176 Cinema B
178 Journl A
179 Journl B

SOCIAL STUDIES
215 SS 10R
225 SS 11R
230 Con Ed A
231 Con Ed B
235 Adv Eco A
255 Adv Gov B
265 Soc Prob A
266 Soc Prob B
278 SS Elect

SCIENCE
310 Bio Sc
315 Bio
320 Gen Chem
325 Chem
330 Gen Phys
335 Physics

MATHEMATICS
400 Math 9
415 Math 10
455 Int Alg
435 Math 11
425 Math 12
445 Math 12S
465 Math 13

PHYSICAL ED
910 Boys 10
911 Boys 11/12
913 Girls 10
914 Girls 11/12
916 PE Makeup B
917 PE Makeup G

LANGUAGE
502 French 1
512 French 2
522 French 3
532 French 4
505 Latin 1
515 Latin 2
525 Latin 3
535 Latin 4
509 Span 1
519 Span 2
529 Span 3
539 Span 4

ART
801 Studio 1A
802 Studio 1B
803 Studio 2A
804 Studio 2B
805 Ceramics A
806 Ceramics B
807 Dra & Pa A
808 Dra & Pa B
809 Sculpt A
810 Sculpt B

INDUSTRIAL ARTS
701 IA 10
700 IA 9AB A
710 IA 10AB B
715 IA 10 A
716 IA 10 B
720 P Tech A
725 Aut Tech B
726 A-S Tech B
727 Woods 1A
728 Woods 1B
730 Metals 1A
732 Metals 1B
750 A-T-Res 1A
751 A-T-Res 2B
760 Electron B
765 Graphics 1A
767 Graphics 2B
721 Mech Dr 1A
724 Mech Dr 2B
731 Mech Dr 3A
735 Mech Dr 4B
702 Hm Maint A

MUSIC
875 Band
895 Choir
880 Rudi A
881 Harm B
890 M. Appre

HOME ECONOMICS
811 Hm Ec 10A
812 Hm Ec 10B
814 Hm Ec 11A
815 Hm Ec 11B
817 Hm Ec 4
824 Hm Ec 6
845 Hm Ec 12
844 Hm Ec 2

GUIDANCE
770 Coop Ed
771 W/S
772 M'Ville
773 _____

BUSINESS ED
612 Intro Bus
615 Type 1
625 Type 2
631 P Typ A
632 P Typ B
633 P-S-I
614 C Math R
610 C Math NR
626 Rec Keep
627 BKP 1
628 BKP 2
629 Shthd 1
638 Shthd 2
639 Transcrip
657 Data Pro
650 Sec Prac
660 Off Prac
655 Com Law

HEALTH
938 Health A
939 Health B

VOC SCH 11
781 Aut Mech
782 Ag Mech
783 Aut Body
784 Bldg Trades
780 Bldg Maint
785 Child Care
786 Conserv
787 Cosmotol
788 Health Sv
789 Trade Cook

VOC SCH 12
792 Aut Mech
793 Ag Mech
794 Aut Body
791 Bldg Maint
795 Bldg Trade
796 Child Care
797 Conserv
798 Cosmotol
799 Health Sv
790 Trade Cook

Figure 4-7
Student Course Request Sheet

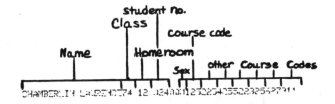

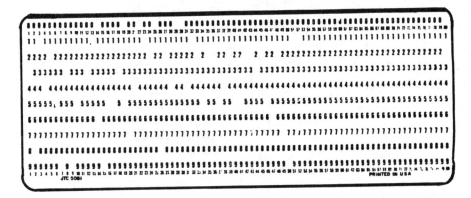

Figure 4-8
Data Processing Card

Room Schedule Board

A room chart is simply a chart for each room in the building on which the scheduler will identify the use of the facility. The chart looks just like the student schedule because it reflects the six-day cycle with all the mods per day. As the scheduler places a course on the board and on the teacher's schedule it is simultaneously placed on the room chart. This assures control of proper room utilization. It also serves as a check on the scheduling process since it prevents the over-scheduling of any room or block of rooms.

Teacher schedules and room schedules should be posted on separate boards. This will allow the schedulers to get a quick glance at a teacher's schedule which will often help in determining where a course should go.

Master Schedule Board

The hub of the scheduling operation is the master schedule board. This board can be made of almost any material, preferably something on which changes can be made readily with little damage to the board itself. A magnetic board, about 6' by 4', is more than adequate for a medium-sized

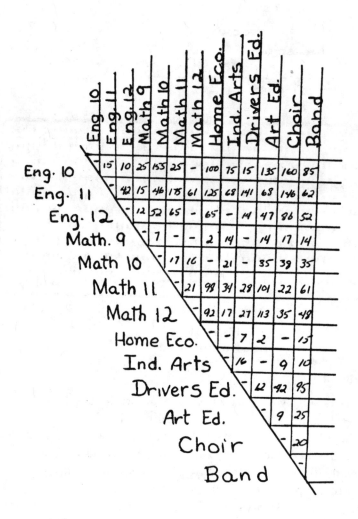

	Eng. 10	Eng. 11	Eng. 12	Math 9	Math 10	Math 11	Math 12	Home Eco.	Ind. Arts	Drivers Ed.	Art Ed.	Choir	Band
Eng. 10		15	10	25	153	25	-	100	75	15	135	160	85
Eng. 11			42	15	46	18	61	125	68	141	68	146	62
Eng. 12				12	52	65	-	65	-	14	47	86	52
Math. 9					7	-	-	2	14	-	14	17	14
Math 10						17	16	-	21	-	35	39	35
Math 11							21	98	34	28	101	22	61
Math 12								92	17	27	113	35	49
Home Eco.									-	7	2	-	15
Ind. Arts										16	-	9	10
Drivers Ed.											42	42	95
Art Ed.												9	25
Choir													20
Band													-

Figure 4-9
Conflict Matrix

school. The board should be large enough to accommodate all the courses in the curriculum. However, in very large schools with many offerings and multi-sections, it need be big enough to hold only the large groups, regular classes, and labs. Small groups may be placed directly on the individual teacher schedules. Some large schools have used an entire wall for their complete schedule; this is fine if you have the room in which to work. Most schools cannot afford that much space for such a purpose.

S T U D E N T   R E Q U E S T

NORWICH SENIOR HIGH SCHOOL

COURSE CODE	TOTAL MALES	TOTAL FEMALES	TOT	TOT	TOT	TOTAL REQUESTS
110 Mess	43	38	80	1		81
115 Eng 10R	95	126	220	1		221
116 Bus Eng	2	32	31	3		34
120 Core	49	41		89	1	90
125 Eng 11R	85	88		170	3	173
130 Eng 12NR	50	54		3	101	104
135 Eng 12R	72	62			134	134
145 Gr Idea A	5	7			12	12
146 Gr Idea B	6	7			13	13
175 Cinema A	14	17		8	23	31
176 Cinema B	14	20		7	27	34
178 Journal A	3	9	1		11	12
179 Journal B	3	3			6	6
215 Soc. S. 10R	127	127	221	1	1	223

Figure 4-10
Tally Sheet

The board itself should be divided equally into the number of day cycles on the vertical scale and the number of mods in the day on the horizontal scale. Then the number of key rooms (or all the rooms if you have space) should be designated at the top border of the first "day" column. This should now be repeated for each of the days in the day cycle.

MASTER SCHEDULE BOARD

Administrative Review of All Data

Because of the mass of data compiled so far, it is worthwhile taking one last look at the operation before going full swing into scheduling. On the wall in the center of the scheduling room should be a master schedule board broken down into the day cycle and mods. Each day cycle has a heading of all or the most important rooms including large group rooms, special labs, etc., to be used. On another wall hangs the faculty schedule

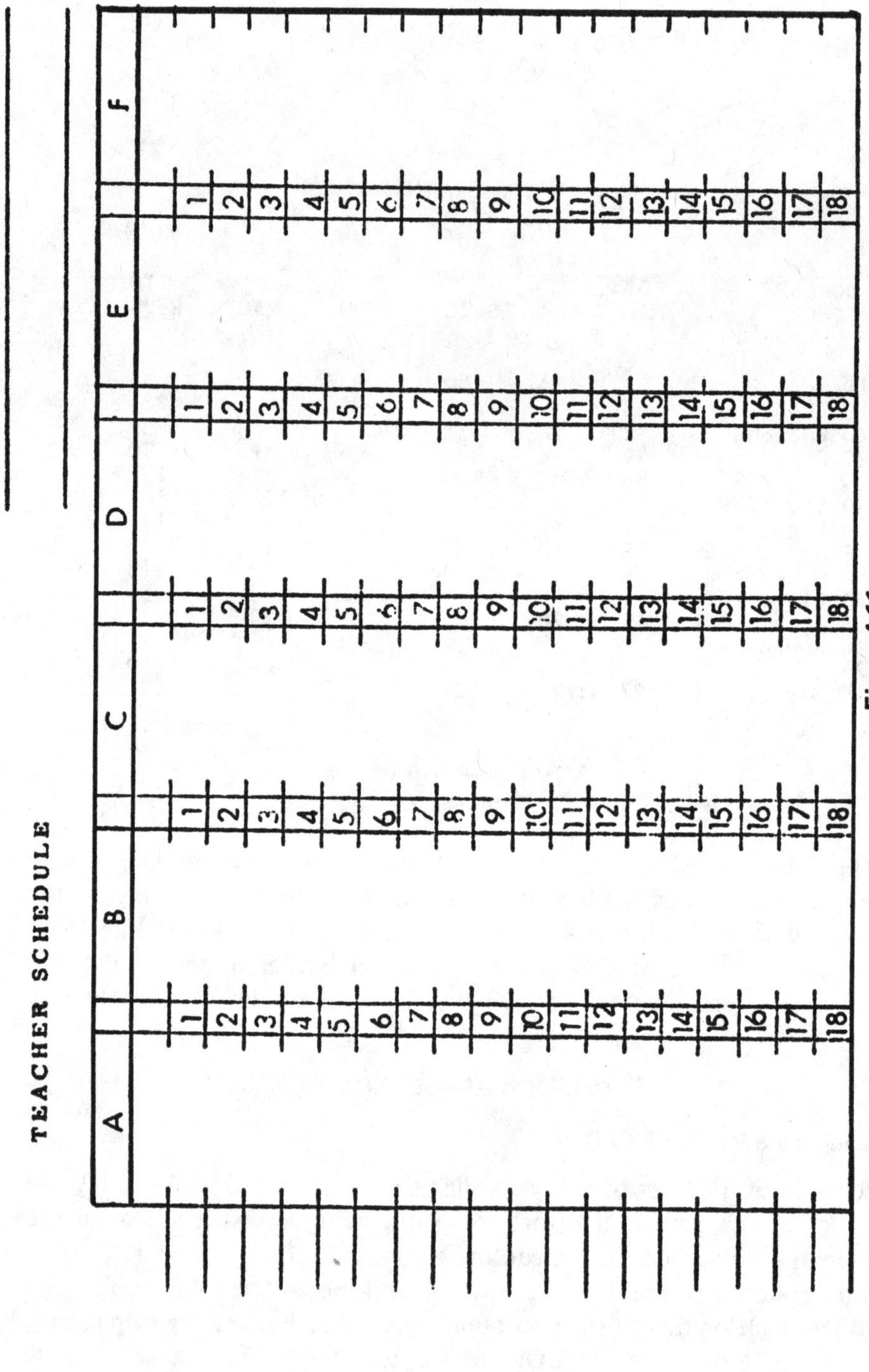

Figure 4-11
Teacher Schedule

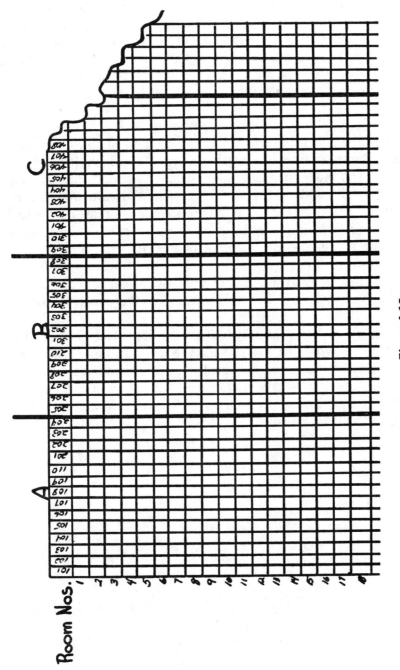

Figure 4-12
Master Schedule

board, and on the third wall is the room schedule board. Somewhere near at hand is a conflict matrix which will be referred to continuously. Close by are the original course configuration sheets with their pertinent data about important restrictions and other memoranda. Finally, in the hands of the scheduling team is the deck of phase cards, each ranked in a scheduling priority, with the appropriate tags, ready to go.

Summary

The initial step in beginning to build the master schedule is to transpose all the data received from the teacher's course configuration sheets to phase cards. Each mode of instruction is discreetly handled: large groups, regular classes, labs, and small groups. The phase cards are then ranked in their order of priority in the scheduling process. The number a particular course mode receives is determined by several factors which together determine the ranking assigned to that phase. Once the numbering has been done, the scheduling team has a single deck of priority cards which they will schedule, one at a time, on the master schedule board. When each phase of each course has been scheduled, the master schedule is completed.

In order to do this job, the scheduling team needs several other "tools of scheduling" to work with. These include a good room to work in, a master schedule board, room and faculty scheduling boards, scheduling labs, and the conflict matrix and course tally sheet. Once these are assembled and all the data has been reviewed by the administration, the school scheduling team is ready to go to work.

5

Building the Master Schedule: Part II

Choosing a place to begin

All the tools for the scheduling procedure have been assembled and it is time to go to work. An administrator faced with the prospect of building a master schedule by hand might well ask, "But where do I begin?" This is especially true if he is one of the modern breed of secondary principals who have never had the experience of building even a conventional schedule manually but have always had the services of the local data processing center—or, at least, last year's schedule to work from.

Following established priorities

The basic operation is simple enough. You take each card in the priority deck, one card at a time, and place the attached tags on the master schedule board until all the phase cards have been scheduled. Each phase card with its respective mode of instruction receives careful consideration and deliberation before it is placed on the master schedule board. The scheduling team begins with priority card one—because this course as previously determined is the most difficult to schedule. Using the school band as an example,[1] the scheduling team will consider all the factors that might influence its meeting time in the school day.

---

[1]This example assumes that the school band is built into the daily schedule and is not an extracurricular activity which takes place before or after the regular school session.

The selection of the band as priority one has been previously discussed but its placement in the master schedule is based on the unique circumstances that are different in each school. Questions which must be dealt with include: Does the choir use the same room? Does the band continue its practices after school? Does the band need to dovetail with the vocational school students' schedule? Does the school have some historical basis for the band's placement in the schedule? Are there other special factors that would help dictate its placement? Once the scheduling team has discussed all the circumstances and has decided where the band will be scheduled, the team member responsible for the master schedule board takes the tags off the phase card and carefully places them on the appropriate spots on the scheduling board (Figure 5-1). The tag color would be that assigned to a mixed group and it would carry the number of students from each grade level—also taken from the course tally sheet. Perhaps mods 16, 17, 18, and days A, C, E are selected. Your first course is now scheduled and you move on to priority number two.

Again the scheduling team must thoroughly discuss the variables that affect the placement of a course on the master schedule. Because the highest priorities are also the most important—large groups, mixed groups, singletons, special programs—the schedulers should not be deceived by the fact that they are faced with an empty board on which it is easy to find room for each course. A mistake in placement on priority #7 may not lead to any real difficulties until you reach priority #75. The scheduling now settles to a routine. Decisions continue to be made, tags are taken off phase cards and placed on the scheduling board as the schedulers move, one by one, through the priority deck.

The temptation to stray from the priority deck will be great. As scheduling progresses, new insights continue to take place, but the schedulers should resist any attempt to deviate from the established priority ranking. Since the variations can be endless, a firm decision must be made to stick with the priority ranking throughout the scheduling.

Scheduling rooms and teachers

Each time the course tags are placed on the master schedule board a recording on the teacher's schedule and the room schedule is made (Figure 5-2). It is extremely important that this is done simultaneously. A mistake on the use of a room or on a teacher's schedule can cost dearly in time and effort at a later date. The task itself is not difficult but it is vital. As the schedule begins to grow in number of courses and sections scheduled, the scheduling team will increasingly refer to the "rooms available" or "teacher availability" factor in determining where any one course fits on the schedule.

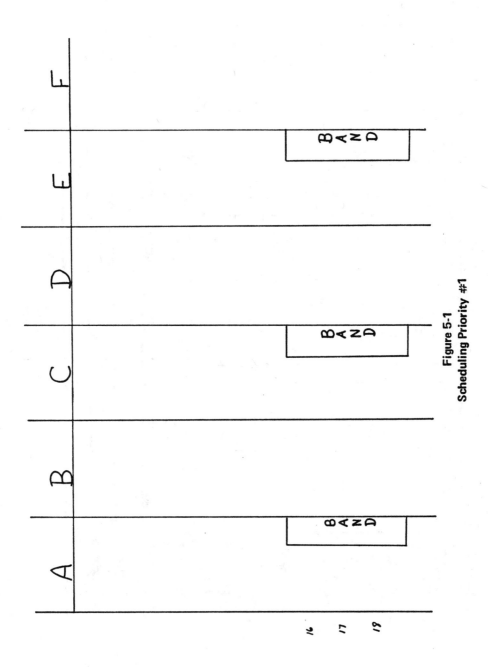

Figure 5-1
Scheduling Priority #1

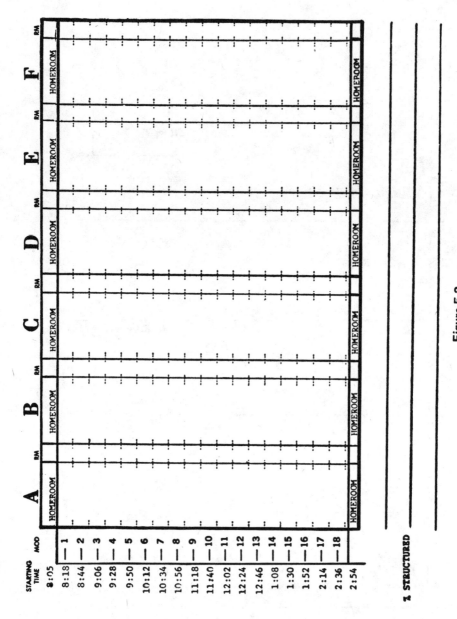

Figure 5-2
Room Schedule

Factors affecting location of course offerings

Each school is different in the factors and variables that affect the positioning of courses in the schedule. This is one of the important considerations in developing the master schedule by hand, because the number of local options and inputs that must be considered far outweighs the restrictions that can reasonably be placed on a computer generated schedule.

However, there are some general parameters that can be considered and when building a schedule. Schedulers should be cognizant of the following important restraints and take them into account: vocational school students; early release for church school; limitations of large groups and small group rooms; scheduling of speciality class rooms such as chemistry or business rooms; student distribution factors; specific individual faculty requirements;[2] half time or shared teachers; the constraint of being cramped in available classroom space, etc.

Bear in mind that most administrators are conversant with their local problems and it is difficult to think of all of them until you actually begin to schedule. Programming a computer for these variables, and for the many others that will come along from restraints imposed by faculty in their course configuration sheets, will perhaps require more of the computer than it is able to perform. Although not all of the above restraints affecting the location of courses may be satisfied, each will have to be dealt with in order to determine the most rational location for each course.

As the schedule is being developed special attention will have to be paid to individual teacher schedules. The schedules must consider such constants as adequate lunch time and preparation time for each teacher. Most faculties, except in the most rigid situations, will accept varying arrangements from day to day. In a school where a period of free prep time is required, it is usually acceptable to have two mods, even though they might not be consecutive, serving this purpose. It also often happens that lunch will vary from day to day but as long as the time is within respectable bounds this should not be a problem. Normally, faculties who are involved in the decision-making process leading to the acceptance of FMS, and versed in its advantages, will understand that this will be the case. Naturally where such flexibility does not exist, this becomes a scheduling constraint.

---

[2] Although as a rule you would prefer not to have faculty tied into one classroom, sometimes the school is bound into contractual obligations. It also happens that most faculties have at least one or two members who, because of a specific physical disability or their senior status, would prefer not to have to travel from class to class.

TRICKS FOR AVOIDING PITFALLS

As you might expect in such a complex operation, there are a number of tricks of the trade to help the scheduling team avoid scheduling pitfalls. Three such "tricks" are the establishment of *day sequences, mod blocking* and *straight line scheduling*.

Day sequences

Day sequences involve the scheduling of combinations of courses so that they may dovetail or interlock with other courses in the schedule. An example would be scheduling courses that meet every other day (three-day sequence) to meet either

         A   C   E
or
         B   D   F

If it is a two-day sequence it could be scheduled either

         A   C
               C   E
         A   E

or

         B   D
               D   F
         B   F

This will allow those courses with two- or three-day sequences to be pieced together more readily on the scheduling board.

Mod blocking

Another scheduling hint, mod blocking, refers to the grouping of mods using informal barriers to guide the schedules. These barriers are set up so that courses may be scheduled within a grouping. (See Figure 5-3.)

This will help prevent overlapping of courses by one or more mods, causing unnecessary conflicts. Illustrated in Figure 5-4 (on left) is a four-mod bio lab scheduled mods 2, 3, 4, 5, which conflicts with a French regular class meeting schedule mod 5. On the right are the same classes scheduled without a conflict.

The barrier lines serve only as guides to keep the schedulers on the right track and reduce overlapping of classes which cause many of the single mod conflicts.

```
                          1    _____
                          2
                          3
    Barrier               4
                               _____
                          5
                          6
                          7
    Barrier               8
                               _____
                          9
                         10
                         11
    Barrier              12
                               _____
                         13
                         14
                         15
    Barrier              16
                               _____
                         17
                         18
```

Figure 5-3

Straight line vs. scatter scheduling

There are two schools of thought with regard to the consistency used in scheduling classes, labs and small groups across the board rather than scatter scheduling. By scheduling classes across the board in the same mods on each meeting date, (straight line scheduling), the schedulers maintain some semblance of daily consistency. The rationale is that there is so much variation in the six-day cycle and other aspects of Flexible Modular Scheduling that this consistency is an advantage. It will tend to reduce student's forgetting to meet their classes because of confusion. It helps students to memorize their schedules so that they do not have to be dependent on a piece of paper or a card. Others who favor scatter scheduling argue that it helps to contribute to the breaking up of the monotony of the schedule, a definite objective of an FMS program, and that it adds to the more rational placement of classes to avoid conflicts. In view of the high rate of conflicts with both the administrator-designed and the computer-generated schedules, it is questionable whether this method has had any greater success. If you use a computer-generated schedule, you have no choice. If you develop the master schedule by hand the

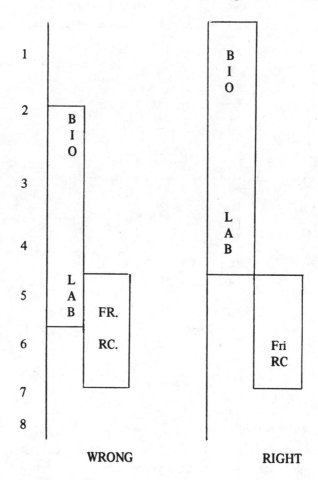

	WRONG	RIGHT

choice is yours; you can move to either extreme, or take a pragmatic middle position.

Many people in the business feel that it is generally helpful if the regular classes and small groups are scheduled simultaneously. This allows for a consistent scheduling pattern, where the classes tend to meet at the same time each day, rather than scattering classes all across the board. The advantage of this pattern is simply that it reduces the number of student "cuts" and "mistakes" that are made. Always somewhat a minor problem in a modular schedule, the variations tend to confuse some students. Scatter scheduling, perhaps more rational from a technical scheduling standpoint, does tend to force the student to a greater reliance on an "in hand" copy of his schedule. This is one of those philosophical choices with practical implications which are left to the discretion of the school administrators.

Adjustments of configurations

From time to time as the work progresses, the scheduling team will encounter difficulty in attempting to schedule a course configuration request. The problem will perhaps be the sequence in which the various modes were requested, the length or frequency of a mode, or just the fact that for some reason the combination of mods is not compatible with other courses scheduled. It could be that the course priority is in the lower range so that a unique course design cannot be handled and the course needs a higher priority. Whatever the reason, problems will arise. It is then imperative for the scheduling team to sit down with the designers of the configuration and the department chairman or any person involved and begin an adjustment process. Often the adjustment is only a mod or a minor change in the sequence. Rarely does it involve a major change. In fact, the priority given to satisfying the staff course configuration requests is usually of such high order that tampering with them is not done unless there truly is no other choice.

Sometimes the adjustments may result in improving the course configuration or meeting pattern. The schedulers, because of their growing familiarity with the entire schedule, may see advantageous adjustments which, after consultation with the faculty, can lead to a stronger course configuration. Other times the adjustment may not be desirable from the teacher's point of view, although experience shows that this is seldom the case.

Scheduling compromises

Part and parcel of this adjustment process is the need to compromise on all phases of schedule building. Remember that in a traditional schedule, when there was a conflict, there was a head-on collision. Not so in a modular schedule. Increased course offering and selections by students, variable time and meeting patterns, and the loss of that nice "even" balance of students assigned and unassigned each period are no longer factors. The imbalance in the flexible schedule causes some overlapping and requires adjustments which lead to some necessary scheduling compromises. The administrative scheduling team arbitrates the compromises and calls in the parties affected. This section is not meant to overplay the need for adjustments and scheduling compromises as a serious problem but rather to call to the attention of the school administrator that this might have to be done. The same is true in a computer-generated schedule. If courses are not properly drawn, this will show up in the loading process when there will be some courses overloaded with students, some partially filled, and some which not a single student can enter. Course configurations carefully drawn and reviewed, along with the experience and expertise of the schedulers, will head off most of the problems.

Periodic tallying of seats available

In a modular schedule the number of students unassigned each mod of the school day and cycle will fluctuate widely. Although this will not happen often, the school should be prepared to be able to handle as high as 50 percent of the students unassigned any given mod of the school day during the cycle. There will also be mods when only 2.3 percent of the students will be free any given day. Although these represent the extremes, the schedulers will have to work at trying to achieve some balance between the average number of students unassigned. A school 65 to 70 percent scheduled on an average would leave some 30 to 35 percent of the student body unstructured. This is a reasonable objective to strive for, although schools concerned about too much student free time can schedule more closely.

All that needs to be done is to take a simple tally from the scheduling tags. This can be done for each mod during the cycle. Unfortunately this represents a time-consuming but necessary task. Since this is just a rough estimate, it should be done several times as the schedule progresses so that some rough data is provided to the schedulers to keep the number of students in balance.

It is also necessary to have the proper number of seats available for each grade level. Too many sophomore classes made available during a given mod would lead to such problems as not enough students available for the courses scheduled. Conversely, too few seats (classes) made available would fill the Commons and resource rooms with sophomores. This is accomplished by using the periodic tally and counting the number of students from each grade level scheduled. This will give the schedulers a rough estimate of the number of seats available each mod.

Distribution and density of faculty

During the construction of the master schedule and as individual faculty schedules are being built, note should also be taken of the distribution and density scheduling of the faculty. There is a definite relationship between how tightly or loosely the faculty is scheduled and its effect on student density. It will also have a relationship to the number of faculty members available for supervision assignments.

If the faculty is scheduled too tightly a problem may arise with the staffing of the area resource centers and the number of students who are absorbed in the individualized instruction phase of the program. This could be critical, because if the faculty on a given mod is tied up with a number of small groups which do not absorb many students, the number of unassigned students may jump very high while the number of faculty available to work with them, run mini-courses or supervise may be very small. Thus, careful consideration to faculty density scheduling is necessary.

Duty rosters can also present a problem if proper faculty distribution is not considered. For schools with teacher aids or supervisory personnel this is no problem. In most schools where the teachers still are responsible for the supervision of lunch rooms and student centers, this becomes very important. Of greatest concern is providing for personnel around the lunch hour. If not enough teachers are unassigned and those that are free are taking their lunch, the administration could experience a problem. Again, this is not a difficult task but it must be given some attention.

For those administrators who have preferences in both faculty and student density scheduling, designing a master schedule by hand holds considerable advantage. The schedules may, by design, slant the heaviest density to the morning, midday, or afternoon at will. For example, one year at Norwich it was considered important to schedule students heavily in the afternoon. Thus faculty scheduling in the morning was kept light. This freed students who seemed to work on individualized instruction projects more effectively in the morning than later in the school day. Another year of scheduling saw the school shift to lighter scheduling around the lunch hour to reduce the one-mod lunch period which many students had. This, in turn, was later found to be a problem because it ended up giving too many students too long a period during the midday. Still another year's scheduling experience resulted in the improvement of this factor.

Although these are not decisive factors on which a school administrator would chose hand scheduling over computer-generated scheduling, such advantages as selective area density scheduling can take care of some ongoing nagging organization problems—to everyone's benefit. The reader should understand that all schedules have their shortcomings. It is the constant refinement in scheduling that results in growth and organizational improvement.

Inclusion of all faculty
and administrative requests

At the scheduling team's right-hand side while the master schedule is being built are all the teachers course configuration requests sheets.

Remember that these included the restrictions and limitations as well as special requests: biology wants a set-up mod and another for breakdown for each large group; social studies wants to have all small groups after a large group and before any other mod is scheduled, plus a host of similar requests. Also proper planning time must be included for all the team-taught sections. No request is too small to be considered if the schedule is to deliver on all those advantages which were discussed earlier. Knocking a team's planning time request down to once a cycle when they had asked for three such meetings might not seem serious at this point in the game to the schedulers, but to the prospective team that was counting on it, this could prove to be a drawback. The schedulers will have to be alert—along with everything else—to see that insofar as possible these faculty requests are met.

Testing the schedule

We are now at the point of making a final check of the schedule to see if it is workable. Actually, the testing has been an ongoing process rather than a culminative activity. From time to time one of the scheduling team has picked a random schedule of one or more of the students in the class being scheduled and tried it out. Ongoing adjustments were made to accommodate difficulties met from this on-the-spot testing. But now the schedule has been completed and the last trial runs take place. A great deal of time and effort has gone into building this master schedule and everyone hopes that it will work well. Soon, when the last step of loading students in the schedule takes place, the entire job will be finalized.

Summary

Building the master schedule manually is a technical, time-consuming task, but anyone can do the job if he follows some established procedures. Priority cards have been ranked and each card must be placed on the master schedule board in its order. There are a range of variables affecting the location of a course in the schedule which are unique and discreet to each school. It is up to a scheduling team of at least two or more members to discuss all the factors which will determine the decision making. Certain pitfalls can be avoided when designing the master schedule through the use of "tricks of the trade." Testing and adjusting the schedule is an ongoing process right to the end. When the master schedule is completed, it is time to load students into the schedule.

6

Loading Students into a
Flexible Modular Schedule

When the members of the hard-working scheduling team have reached the point of loading the students into the schedule, they are almost at the end of the long journey. They can look back with satisfaction at the accomplishment of the difficult task of completing the master schedule—the heart of the flexible scheduling program. The step still before them—loading the students into the schedule—should not be difficult, since the schedule was tested continually while it was being constructed; this will have taken care of the worst "kinks." Because of the complexity of the new schedule and the number of individual decisions that will have to be made, loading in a flexible schedule is more complicated than the routine experienced in a traditional schedule. Nonetheless, it should not be considered a formidable task.

Computer loading

There are, of course, a number of ways to perform this job. Computer companies have become more experienced with all phases of computer scheduling; there are now a number of companies that will perform the separate functions of generating a master schedule or of loading students into an administrator-designed schedule. Westinghouse Learning Corporation, Education Consultants, IBM and other private concerns have excellent loading programs that could save the school administrator a great deal of time. No matter how well the computer program functions, it should be remembered that some time will have to be invested by the guidance and clerical staff to resolve the most difficult conflicts. Nevertheless, for those schools that have the finances (it runs about $1.25 to $1.50 per student) it is well worth the money.

Hand scheduling

For schools that do not have ready access or the necessary finances for computer loading or that would prefer to continue to handle the process manually there is a less expensive but still efficient method for hand loading the students into the master schedule. The techniques have been employed for years, long before computer scheduling came on the scene, and many sophisticated schedules have been loaded by hand.

Personnel for hand loading students

Since a great deal of the job is routine and basically clerical in nature, the school should consider employing some young, part-time people during the summer to do the task. The actual loading, which may be thought of as completing a jig-saw puzzle, requires good mental manipulation. It takes a special type of person for this work. A highly idealistic "social scientist type" would not do the work nearly as well as the logical "mathematics type." This explanation is not meant to preclude any individual but hopefully to serve as a guideline to the administrator in the practical problem of choosing the right kind of people for a very important job.

The number of clerical help to be employed varies widely with the size of the school. Small schools with from 300 to 500 students may need only two people for three to four weeks. Larger schools of 2,000 or more may need four to six schedulers for the entire summer, under the supervision of an experienced guidance person. Norwich, a school of 800, used four schedulers for five weeks. A shorter work day should be considered because the tedium of the work can wear down the scheduler. The task requires a great deal of concentration, and the scheduler's interest and attention span may drop after a long morning. As an average, an inexperienced scheduler should probably schedule about four students an hour. Naturally some students will be scheduled in five minutes. Others with difficult schedules or conflicts which might require individual consultation would require considerably more time. The school administrator should remember that a key advantage to hand scheduling is the opportunity for the schedulers to resolve their problems as they work along. This is true also of student manual loading. As a conflict arises, a student can be reached by phone for a brief discussion, or the student and his parents may have to have an extended consultation with the supervising counselor. Thus, the student's problems are resolved individually as the schedule is loaded. Upon completion of the loading process, when school opens there should be no unresolved conflicts, or students crammed into a course in the last-minute rush—which is, as mentioned before, a major drawback of automated loading programs.

The tools of hand loading

The student loading operation should take place in the scheduling room if at all possible. This will depend on the size of the room, the size and format of the schedule, and so forth, but if it can be done, it is convenient to keep the operations together.

Each loader will work from a set of schedules that represents a completed copy of the master schedule. This will be a schedule of *all* classes, grade by grade, department by department. This schedule is not by teacher but by subject. Thus all social studies classes of the same grade and academic track are on the schedule, indicating the days and time of meetings, modes of instruction, rooms, etc. Each course has a section number assigned which will be used when scheduling is completed and class lists are run on the computer.

Other materials include a stock of empty student schedule sheets, student program request sheets, and pencils with giant erasers. We are now ready to begin scheduling.

The first step is to examine the student course request sheet submitted by guidance after the pupil was interviewed by his counselor. The role of the guidance department in this process cannot be stressed enough. Scheduling students in a flexible schedule is definitely more complex than in a traditional schedule. Many difficult choices will have to be made. Proper course counseling by guidance helps the scheduler determine quickly and accurately which courses are required for the fulfillment of state mandates, sequence, or vocational needs. Beyond that, electives should be clearly marked in order of their priority of interest. Since students usually may take at least one more elective than in a traditional schedule, the counselor should have spent time with the student helping him choose several electives. A good schedule sheet with the appropriate space for important data is included (Figure 6-2).

The second step is for the scheduling team to determine the most difficult class group to schedule. Some schools find freshmen more difficult to schedule than seniors. This will vary with a number of factors:

ENGLISH 10 REGENTS

6 SECTIONS

#	A	B	C	D	E	F
1						
2						
3						
4						
5	SG 101	RC 101-2	RC 101-2	RC 101-2	LG 101-2-3-4-5 6-7-8-9 10-11-12	RC 101-2
6						
7	SG 102					
8						
9	RC 107-8	SG 107	RC 107-8	RC 107-8	SG 108	RC 107-8
10						
11	RC 103-4	RC 103-4	RC 103-4	RC 103-4	SG 103	SG 104
12						
13	RC 109-10	RC 109-10	RC 109-10	RC 109-10	SG 109	SG 110
14						
15	RC 105-6	RC 105-6	RC 105-6	RC 105-6	SG 105	SG 106
16						
17	SG 111	RC 111-12	RC 111-12	RC 111-12	RC 111-12	SG 11...
18						

Figure 6-1
Master Schedule Sheet

STUDENT PROGRAM AS
SUBMITTED BY GUIDANCE

ENGLISH

110 Eng. 10 NR
115 Eng. 10R
116 Business Eng.
120 Eng. 11NR
125 Eng. 11R
130 Eng. 12NR
135 Eng. 12R
145 Gr. Ideas A
146 Gr. Ideas B
175 Cinema A
176 Cinema B

SOCIAL STUDIES

210 SS 10NR
215 SS 10R
220 SS 11NR
225 SS 11R
230 Con. Ed. A
231 Con. Ed. B
235 Economics A
255 Advanced Gov't B
265 Social Problems A
266 Social Problems B

MATHEMATICS

400 Math 9
415 Math 10
425 Math 11
435 Math 12A
445 Math 12B
455 Int. Alg.
465 Math 13

PHYSICAL EDUCATION

910 Boys P.E. A
911 Boys P.E. B
912 Boys P.E. C

913 Girls P. E. A
914 Girls P. E. B
915 Girls P. E. C

HEALTH

938 Health A
939 Health B

SCIENCE

310 Bio. Sc.
315 Bio
320 Gen. Chem.
325 Chem.
330 Gen. Phys.
335 Physics

LANGUAGE

502 French
512 French 2
522 French 3
532 French 4

505 Latin 1
515 Latin 2
525 Latin 3
535 Latin 4

509 Spanish 1
519 Spanish 2
529 Spanish 3

ART

810 Studio 1A
802 Stuidio 1B
803 Studio 2A
804 Studio 2B
805 Ceramics A
806 Ceramics B
807 Dra & Pa A
808 Dra & PA B
809 Schlpture A
810 Sculpture B

DRIVER ED.

941 Theory A
951 Theory B

INDUSTRIAL ARTS

700 IA 9AB
710 IA 10AB

715 IA 10A
716 IA 10B

720 P. Tech A
725 Aut.Tech E
726 A-S Tech B
727 Woods 1A
728 Woods 2B
730 Metals 1A
732 Metals 2B
750 A-T-Res 1A
751 A-T-Res 2B
760 Electronics B

765 Graphics 1A

767 Graphics 2B

721 Mech Dr. 1A
724 Mech Dr. 2B
731 Mech Dr. 3A
735 Mech Dr. 4B

MUSIC

875 Band
876 Percussion
877 Brass
878 Woodwind
879 Stage Band
885 Orchestra
895 Choir
896 Select Choir
880 Rudiments A
881 Harmony B
890 Music Apprec.

BUSINESS ED.

615 Typing I
625 Typing II
631 Pers. Typ. A
632 Pers. Typ. B.
614 Com. Math R
610 Com. Math NR

626 Rec. Keep.
627 Bkkp. I

629 Shthd. I

638 Shthd. II
639 Transcrp.

657 Data Pro.

650 Sec. Prac.

660 Off. Prac.

655 Comm. Law

CO-OP ED.

770 Co-Op Ed.

VOC. SCHOOL

781 Voc Sch. A
782 Voc Sch. B

WORK-STUDY
791 W/S

HOME ECONOMICS
811 Hm. Ec. 10A
812 Hm. Ec. 10B
814 Hm. Ec. 11A
815 Hm. Ec. 11B
816 Hm. Ec. 6A
817 Hm. Ec. 6B
824 Hm. Ec. 2
844 Hm. Ec. 4
845 Hm. Ec. 12B

Figure 6-2
Student Data Sheet

state law, class size, local school policies with respect to curriculum, vocational interests, academic or nonacademic pursuits, etc. Perhaps the choice will be junior vocational students who attend the area occupational center and are thus in school only half the day. Since they must, as a rule, complete their English, social studies and physical education requirements, these students need to be scheduled first. Once identified, each scheduler takes a batch of course request sheets and begins to schedule each student, one by one, until all the students in the group are scheduled. Since some preliminary trial scheduling has taken place during the process of building the schedule it should be anticipated that many of the students will fit in immediately. Others, as previously discussed, may require more attention and some will have conflicts that need to be resolved.

Tally Sheet

The loading team should attempt to distribute the students as evenly as possible in all the sections. To meet this end, a tally sheet is at hand in the room; as each student is loaded into a section the tally is recorded (Figure 6-3). In this manner early problems are identified. It will be immediately apparent to the scheduling team that certain sections become over-loaded, while others are virtually empty. This information can be translated immediately into adjustments to the master schedule. Often it is only the misplacing of a mod or two that can make the difference between students getting into a class or having a conflict. However, sometimes the process of loading students shows serious flaws in the schedule. In that case the appropriate work will need to be done.

The tally sheet also serves as a control on the scheduling of students so that the loaders can try to arrange balanced classes. Sometimes one section of a course will fill up quickly compared to other sections. When this happens, some important decisions must be made. It is helpful to ask questions such as "What's causing this to happen?" and "How can we adjust the other sections to accomodate more students?" Sometimes a section is closed, leaving students who were counting on entering that particular section with conflicts. This problem can be solved by rescheduling other persons out of the section, thus making room for the first students. This is another advantage of the manual loading process. In a computer run, once a student is loaded into a schedule the machine cannot take him out later and reassign him to make room for others. These decisions are made not by the loaders but by their interaction with the guidance personnel and the scheduling team, who are there to supervise the project.

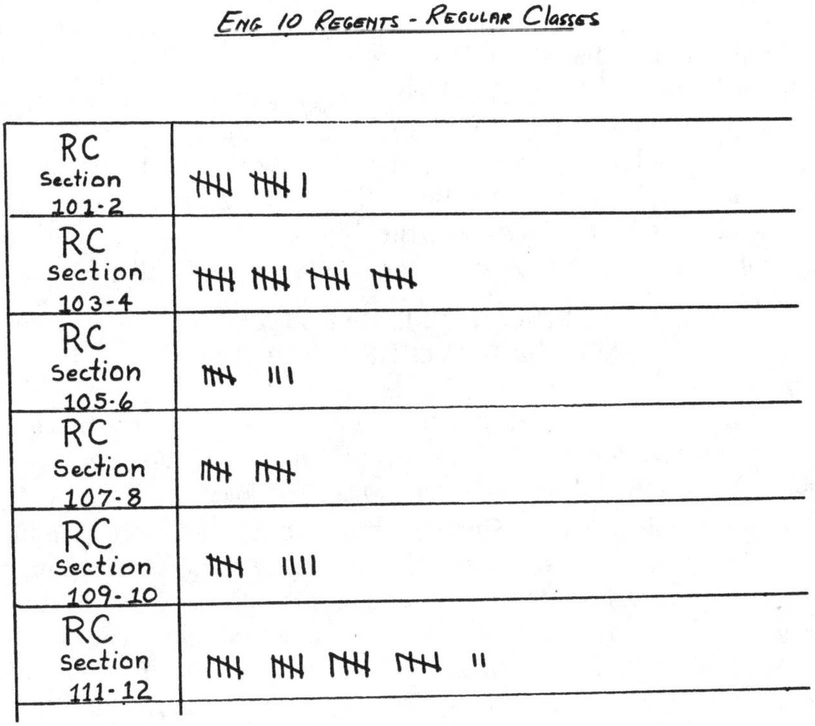

ENG 10 REGENTS - REGULAR Classes

RC Section 101-2	⊬⊬ ⊬⊬ I
RC section 103-4	⊬⊬ ⊬⊬ ⊬⊬ ⊬⊬
RC section 105-6	⊬⊬ III
RC Section 107-8	⊬⊬ ⊬⊬
RC section 109-10	⊬⊬ IIII
RC section 111-12	⊬⊬ ⊬⊬ ⊬⊬ ⊬⊬ II

Figure 6-3
Tally Sheet

Frequently these can be identified early and corrected before any damage is done. Unlike a computer schedule where each run must be complete before you can redesign or shift courses, loading students by hand allows the scheduling team to adjust the schedule as they move to the eventual goal of the operation—each student with a fully scheduled program in a master schedule that serves the needs of almost all the students.

Working Out Individual Problems

Throughout the previous chapters it has been stated that one of the most important advantages of scheduling manually is that it allows for greater individualization in student programming. This can be seen most clearly by going through some scheduling procedures. Student A, a sophomore, has course requests for English 10R*, World History (SS10R) French, Biology, Geometry (Math 10), Physical Education and Graphics. The first step for the loader is to take a blank student schedule from which he will work. He also has a copy of the master schedule in front of him. The trick in scheduling by hand is to begin with the same set of priorities in loading individual students as you used blocking in the courses on the master schedule. Begin by placing the large group sections on the student schedule sheet and then move on to the multiple section going from the singletons to those having the greatest number of offerings.

STUDENT SCHEDULE SHEET
LARGE GROUP MEETINGS SCHEDULED

From this point the loader usually begins to sense certain patterns developing and can take these into account as he loads students into the proper large groups—where there is a choice. The loading of a student into large groups is fairly simple. Since most schools have no more than one or two large group rooms the scheduling of classes into these rooms has usually been well distributed. When building the master schedule it might be useful to keep in mind the scheduling of related large groups such as the same grade English and Social Studies in such a manner that it will cause the least amount of conflicts. For example they might be scheduled the same mods on alternate days.

As in all student scheduling the placement of a course has implications for all others. Therefore even though the student schedule is a blank when you begin loading, it is still necessary to give careful consideration to the placement of each large group.

Scheduling Regular Classes,
Small Groups and Labs

After scheduling all of the student's large groups the loader can now begin blocking in the rest of the student's schedule. This includes all the regular classes, small groups and labs for each section the student is assigned except in those courses where the classroom teacher will schedule the student the first day of school. Again the same process repeats itself: first priority is given to singletons, then doubletons and difficult combinations which the loader has been able to discern.

---

*Represents a Regents or academic track.

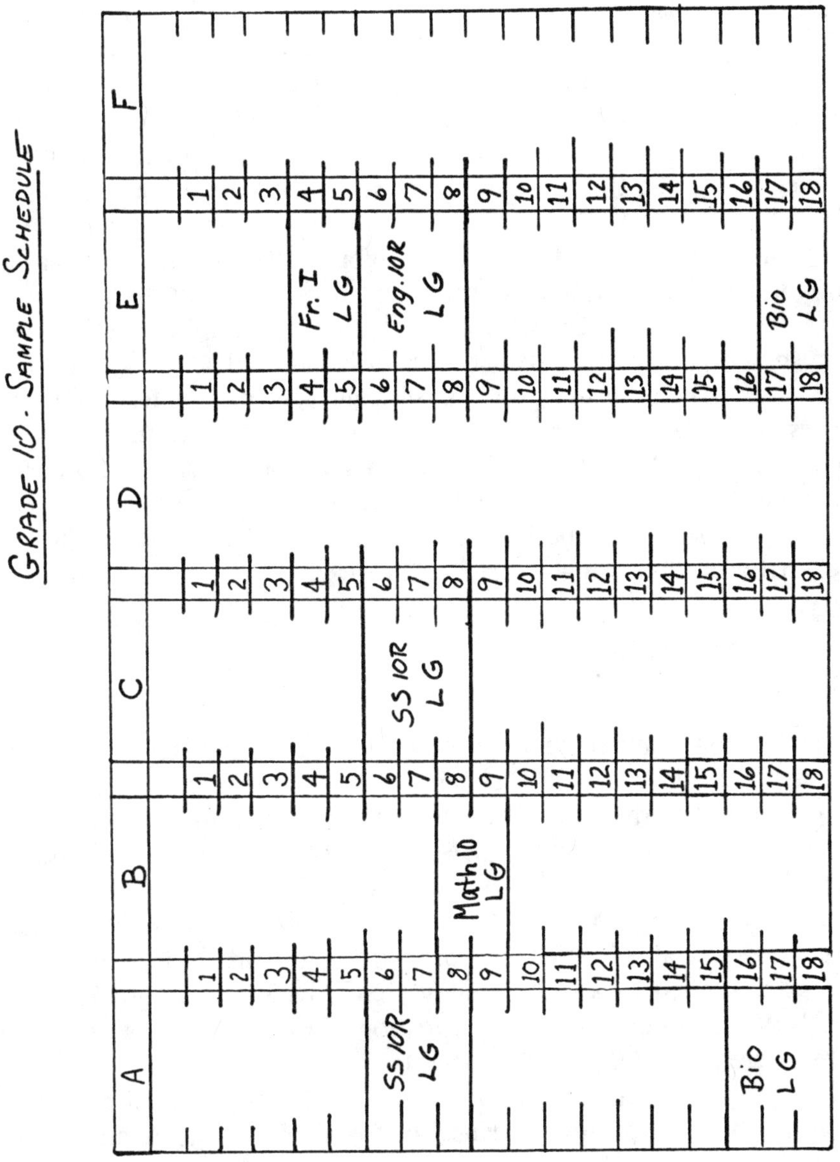

GRADE 10 · SAMPLE SCHEDULE

A		B		C		D		E		F
	1		1		1		1		1	
	2		2		2		2		2	
	3		3		3		3	Fr. I	3	
	4		4		4		4	LG	4	
	5		5	SS 10R	5		5		5	
SS 10R	6	Math 10	6	LG	6		6	Eng. 10R	6	
LG	7	LG	7		7		7	LG	7	
	8		8		8		8		8	
	9		9		9		9		9	
	10		10		10		10		10	
	11		11		11		11		11	
	12		12		12		12		12	
	13		13		13		13		13	
	14		14		14		14		14	
	15		15		15		15		15	
Bio	16		16		16		16	Bio	16	
LG	17		17		17		17	LG	17	
	18		18		18		18		18	

Figure 6-4
Student Schedule Sheet,
Large Group Schedule

REGULAR CLASSES AND LABS SCHEDULED

At this time the placement of sections may become more difficult and the loader may run into his first conflicts. It may be a one mod overlap between a large group and a lab or regular class meeting. Or it might be a greater problem than just a mod conflict.

Note that these are not head-on conflicts and that the student may still spend a majority of the time in both courses. This is unlike the conflicts that exist in a traditional schedule which are either/or conflicts where the student had no choice but to take one course or another. Once school has begun, minor conflicts in a mod schedule are worked out by the student through consultation with the two teachers involved. As an illustration, a student might have a conflict between a Spanish class and a biology lab. If he is weak in the language but strong in biology, it would be feasible for him to miss his bio lab in order that he not miss the Spanish class. The bio lab might then be made up during the student's unassigned time. Another way to handle the conflict would be to rotate the missing mod or even a class on an alternating cycle basis. In any event, a great deal of flexibility is desirable between the pupil and teachers involved.

Establishing priorities in the event of conflicts

Most teachers who understand the program and are not disturbed by an occasional student with a conflict and adjust very easily. However, as a practical guideline for the school administrator who will have to resolve some potentially more difficult conflicts, it would be valuable to establish a priority ranking between modes of instruction. These include, in order of their probable importance to all faculty: (1) large groups, (2) labs, (3) regular classes, and (4) small groups. Setting up this order (or any other order determined by a school), allows initial resolution of almost all the conflicts on opening day. As the year progresses, adjustments can be made to more closely reflect individual needs.

Finally the loader schedules a student into small groups. Small groups have the lowest loading priority because they generally have the greatest number of options in which to slot a student. Most faculty members also tend to permit interchanging of students with other teachers in small groups. This allows the loader even greater flexibility in placing a student. Nevertheless, since small groups have the lowest priority they also have a higher percentage of conflicts than do the other modes.

	A	B	C	D	E	F
	HM RM	HM RM	HM RM	HM RM	HM RM	HM RM
1				P.E.		P.E.
2		P.E.			P.E.	
3	Fr.I RC	914	Fr.I RC	Fr.I SG		
4		Fr.I SG 21		SS 10R	Fr.I LG	Fr.I SG
5	SS 10R LG	SS 10R RC		SG 313		SS 10R RC
6			SS 10R LG		Eng.10R LG	
7	LG					
8	Math 10 RC	Math 10 LG			LG	
9			Math 10 RC	Math 10 RC	Math 10 RC	Math 10 RC
10	406					
11						
12						
13	Eng.10R RC	Eng.10R RC	Eng.10R RC	Eng.10R RC		Eng.10R RC
14						
15						
16	Bio LG					Bio
17		Bio RC	Bio RC	Bio RC	Bio LG	Lab.
18		205				

Figure 6-5
Minor Course Conflict

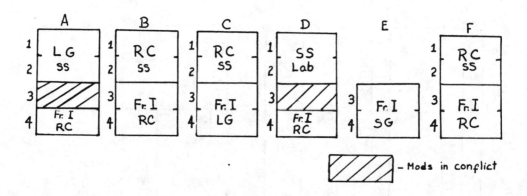

Figure 6-6
Minor Course Conflict

Percentage of time scheduled

Note that the top of the schedule sheet includes notations *#mods* and *% structure*. Each course in the curriculum has a designation of the number of mods it meets. These are totaled by the counselor when the student's course request is being prepared, thus allowing the counselor to determine how much free time the student has available. Since too much unassigned time is unacceptable, a maximum of 35 percent unassigned time is a good goal to shoot for. Based on an 18-mod per day, six-day cycle of 108 mods, a student scheduled 65 percent would be blocked in approximately 76 mods. Students who elect to take more than the minimum number of courses will find themselves structured even more. In any event, a full-time day should have a minimum number of mods scheduled for each student.

Certainly some students have the maturity, intellectual ability or interest to handle more free time than the minimum established. Conversely, there are always those who cannot handle any free time at all. The FMS program permits the school officials, teachers, guidance counselors and administration to work this out on an individual basis later, but at the time of scheduling it is important to have a minimum guide when dealing with an entire student population. It also helps to set the parameters whereby the student and counselor work. At the time of the schedule preparation, this information is compiled by the counselor for the purpose of statistical control over the distribution of students in the program.

Cross tally

About three-quarters of the way through scheduling a cross tally should be taken. This is done by tallying the average number of students scheduled in each grade, as noted on the scheduling tags. This will tell you the number of students scheduled from each grade level (and conversely, the number of students free). From this information you can make decisions about where to place the remaining courses. A final cross tally should be taken when the schedule is complete. This has program implications in that during times of low student scheduling, mini-courses, special assemblies or special resource coverage may be scheduled.

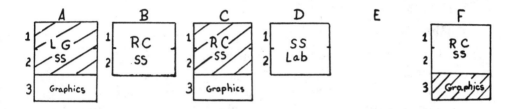

Figure 6-7
Major Course Conflict

Final data output

Once the students have been scheduled and the sections reasonably balanced, the scheduling team is almost finished. Several minor wrap-up activities need to be done before the job is completed. A thorough check of the student schedule, for example, will usually point out occasional errors—mostly in the omission of data such as blocking in a class or putting in a section number. The schedule should now be finalized with all the necessary adjustments made. Except for students who will be arriving late to school, an occasional program change or an honest scheduling mistake, all student schedules are now completed. We are now ready for the run-off of class lists and the distribution of material.

As the student was being scheduled, the courses into which he was being slotted had a data processing number. This is different from the course code number earlier used to derive the conflict matrix. Then there was only one series of digits to indicate the course represented. Now we are interested in both the course and the number of sections it has. The numbers were entered on the student scheduling sheet in the space provided for course and section numbers.

These numbers are now sent to the data-processing center along with the other necessary information. From this the class lists are run. It is a simple procedure, more in the line of information processing than computing. Teachers' names, room numbers and section numbers are all classified and machine collated. The resulting print-out gives a complete breakdown of all information needed for the opening of school: individual print-outs of student schedules with each course, room assignment, and teacher's name recorded; class lists for each teacher in school; and any other information that the school administrator may find convenient. The loading task is now completed and the school should be ready for business.

Costs of hand loading

The direct outlay in costs for a manually loaded schedule varies a great deal, depending mainly on the size of the school. Usually young people will work as loaders for minimum wage or the competitive regional wage for summer employees. In a small school of 300 students, two students working three weeks represent an investment of just $420 (at $2.00 per hour for a 35-hour week). A larger school of 2000 students may need six to eight loaders for as long as six weeks during the summer to do the job. The amount of administrative or guidance service rendered is not included, because these again vary in both price of the personnel and the amount of time they must invest in assisting the loaders. However, considerable time must also be spent by these same people in a computer-loaded schedule.

Time?

How long does it take to construct a schedule? A fair question but difficult to answer. For neophytes, the first time through for a school of 1,000 pupils may take as long as two weeks, working about four hours per day, to complete the schedule. The reason why it is difficult to judge is that the variables affecting the time factor are many. How complicated are the configurations? How many restrictions exist? How quickly can the schedulers schedule? Do they work in an uninterrupted setting (at night or undisturbed) or do they have to contend with daily routine?

With experience and the proper setting, a good team should be able to schedule the same school in less than a week, working four hours per day. Although the schedule is usually constructed from scratch each year, a

Mod	A (HM RM)	B (HM RM)	C (HM RM)	D (HM RM)	E (HM RM)	F (HM RM)
1	I.S.	P.E.	I.S.	P.E.	I.S.	P.E.
2						
3	Fr.I R.C.	Fr.I SG (914)	Fr.I R.C.	Fr.I SG	Fr. Lab	Fr.I SG
4		(521)			Fr.I LG	SS 10R RC
5	I.S.	SS 10R RC	I.S.	SS 10R (313 SG)		
6	SS 10R RC		SS 10R		Eng.10R	
7		I.S.	LG	I.S.	LG	I.S.
8	LG	Math 10 LG		Fr. Lab		
9	Math 10 RC (406)	I.S.	Math 10 RC	Math 10 RC	Math 10 RC	Math 10 RC
10						
11	Lunch	Lunch	Lunch	Lunch	Lunch	Lunch
12						
13	Eng.10R RC	Eng.10R RC	Eng.10R RC	Eng.10R RC	Fr. Lab	Eng.10R RC
14						
15	I.S.	I.S.	I.S.	I.S.	I.S.	Bio Lab
16						
17	Bio LG	Bio RC	Bio RC	Bio RC	Bio LG	
18						

521
406
110
313
205
914

% scheduled

68

A Typical Student Scheduling
Sheet with the Course Numbers
Entered on the Left

French Labs ARE Scheduled BY
Teacher After the Start of School.

Figure 6-8

school may decide, after a number of scheduling experiences, to hold a number of factors constant, thereby reducing the time requirement still further. Also, in smaller schools some group scheduling can be done if the students to be scheduled fit one basic pattern.

Larger schools do not necessarily take much longer to schedule since the distribution of courses in a large school is often much easier. There are fewer singletons or doubletons to be concerned about and generally greater flexibility in staff and room utilization. Smaller schools may be a little more difficult to schedule because of their many restrictions. However, their size will reduce the total time investment to a negligible amount.

Summary

The scheduling team is now entering the last phase of the job of completing an FMS master schedule—loading the students into that schedule. Several commercial companies offer excellent loading programs at a fairly nominal cost. These are specialized to load students into more sophisticated schedules and may be purchased separately from the computer-generated scheduling. Nonetheless, there are several ways a schedule may be loaded manually at real cost savings to the school. Whether computer or manually loading, the process is essentially the same and it is well worth the school administrator's time to become familiar with it.

A schedule may be loaded by employing several young people during the summer to do this mainly clerical task. The schedules are supervised by the administration throughout. The schedulers quickly become familiar with the mechanics of the schedule and are helpful in suggesting necessary adjustments. ·

The one big advantage of manual scheduling is that conflicts can be handled and resolved on an individual basis. Also, since there are usually a number of conflicts in a modular schedule, these must still be resolved by the school staff prior to school opening. An excessive number of students in conflict will make it very difficult for the school to individualize a student's schedule since there just won't be enough time. Finally, hand loading is usually less expensive than the use of commercial computer-loading programs.

7

Interaction Between Students
and Teachers During Unstructured Time

But how can a group "achieve enough maturity to keep itself under control" if its members never have an opportunity to exercise control? Far from helping students to develop into mature, self-reliant, self-motivated individuals, schools seem to do everything they can to keep youngsters in a state of chronic, almost infantile, dependency. The pervasive atmosphere of the distrust, together with rules covering the most minute aspects of existence, teach students every day that they are not people of worth, and certainly not individuals capable of regulating their own behavior.[1]

Why increased unstructured time for students

The most critical element in the modular schedule is the factor of student behavior, for ultimately the success or failure of the program will depend upon it. The modular schedule confronts the student with a wide range of decisions that previously have been out of his reach. The student's area of authority over his own actions widely broadens. How the student reacts to his new situation and how the school organizes itself to meet with this is the key to a successful FMS program.

Of immediate concern in a modular schedule is the increased out-of-class or unstructured time available to all students. It is this factor that

---

[1] Charles E. Silberman, *Crisis in the Classroom* (New York: Random House, Inc., 1970), p. 134.

will have the greatest impact on student behavior. The amount of free time any student has will vary from grade to grade and by major subject areas. However, as mentioned before, a figure of 35 to 40 percent unstructured time out of the total school day can be used as an average. This generally represents a greater amount of unscheduled time for the student than he would find in a traditional schedule. It is in the utilization of this free time that the student gains authority and learns decision-making. Therefore it is important that a variety of alternatives are readily accessible to the student during the school day and that the student be able to move freely to and from these activities during his unstructured time. Furthermore, the student must be recognized by the school authorities as an individual capable of making daily decisions about how to use his time properly. Obviously a program such as this, which allows students some control over certain areas of decision-making, changes the tight student control structure which has developed over the years in most schools.

Actually student discipline in most schools is administratively wasteful and educationally counter-productive. Regulations are designed to control the three to five percent of students who need direct supervision, but they have the effect of controlling all students whether they need it or not. Only the three to five percent who need tight control should have it. The majority of students who demonstrate ongoing, reasonable behavior should be free from these restrictive controls. It is necessary to recognize that order and discipline can be maintained without tight control and that the benefits gained by giving up some of the control outweigh the inconveniences this may bring about.

**Alternate areas for student use
during unstructured time**

Just turning students loose during their unstructured time is easy. But there have been some spectacular failures by schools which, in attempting to move to a modular schedule, did not take cognizance of their responsibility to provide other activities and learning centers for use by students during their free time. Providing students with large amounts of unstructured time should be seen as a facilitating step in student learning and not as any goal of flexible scheduling in itself. The objective is to permit a student to learn how to use his time more effectively and responsibly while still under the guidance of school personnel. The school administration and faculty must be prepared to modify their patterns of working with students to accommodate the new program with its unstructured time. In fact, the success or failure of the program will hinge on the ability of the school personnel to mobilize their resources to create an effective out-of-class school experience. The design of these experiences should involve the use of a variety of alternatives from which the student will be able to choose. These alternatives will vary from school to school depending a great deal, of course, on local conditions, but most schools feature a number of basic options. In describing the alternatives it is not being suggested that these options are only to be found in a flexibly scheduled school. On the contrary, it is well recognized that most schools offer one, more, or even all of the choices being suggested. It is rather that in a flexibly scheduled school these alternatives are fundamental to the program, and a school taking advantage of the increased program flexibility offered by the new schedule must further provide free-time options for its students.

The Commons

This is an area set aside where students can sit and talk and have light snacks. It specifically offers the student the opportunity to "take a break" during the school day.

Since the restructuring of the school minimizes one of the previously held cardinal principles of school scheduling, namely *balancing,* the number of students that are free at any one time in the modular schedule may vary enormously. It is estimated that on some mods during the school week (cycle) as many as 50 percent of the students may be unassigned. Since a student is often free for only a mod between classes, the Commons offers that individual a place to have a snack or just to socialize for a short period. It is also true that some students may have large blocks of unscheduled time available to them. Excessive use of the Commons privilege under that circumstance must be handled. Rules concerning behavior in the Commons vary between schools but are usually held to a minimum and should be enforced by someone who is in charge of supervising the area. The law is very specific in most states that such areas must be supervised either by professional personnel or by aides. As in any such endeavor, most students respond well to this opportunity. It is looked upon as a good chance to take some time out from the stresses and strains of the daily routine. Thus if you have just finished an important math exam it is extremely helpful to have a "mod" break in which to talk things over before going on to your French class.

In every school there is a small percentage of students who do not act responsibly in such an informal environment. They spend unwarranted amounts of time in the Commons and abuse courtesy rules with respect to other people's rights; they obviously do not have the maturity to manifest responsible behavior. These students can lose their privilege of going to the Commons and find themselves structured into a quiet study area much like that in a traditional system. The "penalty" of structuring during unassigned time is a powerful force which actually gives the school administrator more control over pupil behavior than he had before.

It is interesting to note that many students like to work while snacking so that a fairly significant percentage of the students who frequent the Commons are not necessarily "wasting their time." They like the informality of the Commons, can work with noise, and are often engaged in cooperative learning. This working together, which is indeed a very productive form of activity, is facilitated by the informal atmosphere of the Commons.

Although not all students are actually directly engaged in some learning activity, the time spent in the Commons may still be productive. It gives the student a chance to socialize and engage in the activity of communicating. A review of the day's work, the latest notes on a classroom activity, what to prepare for a class or teacher, etc., are all part of institutional communications, a pattern very necessary to the school's clientele. Just as secretaries, teachers, school administrators or any system employee takes the opportunity to exchange ideas, feelings, and news, so students too are part of the system, and an opportunity to exchange information is a vital part of their institutional adjustment. The fact that previously this was done in a more clandestine manner through sneaky conversations, letters, or quick snatches of verbal exchanges while passing from class to class indicates schools have never successfully suppressed this phenomonen.

Many teachers understand and accept the rationale for a Commons with little or no difficulty. They work well with students in the Commons setting, seeming to be able to control them with little effort, feeling secure enough to mingle with them, have a snack with them, and still fulfill their function of controlling the area. Other teachers may not find this so easy. They have a philosophical or personal conflict about seeing students "free," talking, and, to the inexperienced or unaccepting eye, engaged in unproductive behavior. Some teachers might have a basic fear of losing control since students are not seated, by number, in long rows in a structured study assignment. These teachers find interaction with students in the Commons very difficult. They are not adaptable enough to mingle with students and establish relationships based on personality and acceptance in the informal situation rather than the more formal and secure teacher-student relationship of the classroom. A teacher in such a position may feel uncomfortable about the changing nature of the degree of control he or she may have over the group. In the class there is no question about the teacher's authority, whereas the direct control over the larger group is greatly diffused in the Commons. In fact, the teacher has very little control over the entire group and relies mainly on the good judgment and reasonableness of the majority of the students. As supervisor he can exert influence on the few who do not handle themselves well in such an informal setting and talk with them, discipline them or send them to other authorities to have them disciplined. Teachers who have a fairly high tolerance for working with give-and-take situations do well in this setting. Those who tend to be rigid, see things only in simplistic terms, e.g., good, bad, etc., find working in the Commons environment more difficult.

Quiet study

A quiet study supersedes the old study hall but is specially designed for students who come there on a voluntary basis. Quiet study is best situated near the Commons so that students may pass from either area or a resource center as easily as possible. In any event, wherever it is located, it should be in the same place every day for every mod. When first moving to the new schedule at Norwich we did not follow this axiom. Instead, quiet study was in a different room many times during the cycle. Students had to refer to a posted schedule to see where it was any given day. As a result attendance was poor. After we relocated quiet study the following year and gave it a permanent place, students' attendance increased dramatically.

Because students are there voluntarily it makes sense for this area to be covered by an aide rather than by professional staff. This allows teachers greater time to spend with students in the individualized instructional phase of the program rather than expending it on non-productive forms of pupil supervision.

Instruction material center

The day when the classroom teacher was the storehouse and fountain of knowledge from whom all the important information emanated is an idea long obsolete. Most modern schools recognize that the heart of the school learning program is in the research, collection and presentation by the students of data-supported themes and concepts. This *process of learning* has become the focal point of school activity, and the entire faculty and school organization should serve as a large resource center, with its core the Instructional Materials Center. Here is located the cumulative knowledge extant in thousands of volumes of books, films, filmstrips, records, periodicals and other resource materials; a far greater wealth of information than a student could ever be exposed to in the classroom. The challenge, then, is to create a curriculum that makes heavy use of these resources, giving a student wide latitude to investigate areas of interest: to conceptualize viable learning hypotheses based on preliminary investigations; to collect the necessary data; make tentative conclusions; and finally present his findings, either individually or through a group process, to his classmates. The classroom in this kind of program becomes a center of debate, controversy, exploration and testing of ideas. The independent study time that the student gains in the flexible schedule should be used to delve in depth into the materials storage—housed in the Instructional Materials Center.

If the school curriculum has made the proper provision for this kind of learning program and the faculty has internalized and made operative the concept of learning based on research presentation, then student use of the school IMC will be considerable.

The author had the opportunity to visit a large, 1800 pupil, suburban high school in Long Island, N.Y. which had advertised a superior academic curriculum. When he asked the librarian how many students, on the average, were serviced each day, she answered, with a great deal of pride, "Over four hundred." In contrast, Norwich, with a pupil population of 800, approximately a third of whom were terminal, in the first year of the flexible schedule averaged more than 1,000 students each day in the school Instructional Materials Center!

These numbers reflect a marked contrast between two schools in philosophy, *modus operandi,* and goals. In the case of Norwich they show the heavy reliance of the faculty on the new basis for learning. Readers should understand that to develop a resource-based program involves a great deal more planning on the part of the teacher. With a number of individuals and groups engaged in varying activities, moving at different rates of speed and working on differentiated levels of difficulty, the classroom-management role of the teacher changes considerably from that in a traditional structure. To help organize such a program the teachers at Norwich worked with Learning Activity Packages (LAPS), which were first originated at Nova High School in Florida. A LAP is a student-learning packet not unlike the older version of teacher units. It contains the objectives of the area to be covered, contains pretests and post evaluation, and offers the student several alternatives depending on his abilities and interests to reach the LAP objectives. The LAP may include large group and small group work. However, it serves as the pupil's guide to that segment of the course to be studied. These LAPS can be designed so that mandatory or optional activities provide for research-based work. With this approach to curriculum and learning the flexibly scheduled school will assure itself of heavy student and faculty use of the Instructional Materials Center.

Resource centers

Each department should have an established resource area where students may come for personalized help. During a student's unassigned time he should be free to visit the resource center either to work with the assigned personnel or to use the reserve materials in the center. All staff on duty in the resource center can work with any student, giving the student greater exposure to more faculty. The degree of elaborateness of the resource area will depend on the relative wealth of the district and the design of the building. It may vary from a small, formerly custodial area in an old building to a specially designed and equipped resource area in a newer school. In any event, the resource area should be staffed by departmental staff or an aide, and should be open to students as often as possible. Keeping it open all day every day is the ultimate but not always obtainable goal.

The departmental resource area serves as a supplement to the Instructional Materials Center. The department may house certain required books or other material there on loan from the IMC for a special unit. Teachers should arrange to meet students in the resource center for the individualized instruction phase of their program. Students can be asked to visit with a teacher by appointment, or can just drop in to the resource center for tutorial help. It is advisable to translate this phase of the program very carefully to the students. Often they do not understand or are slow to capitalize on the opportunities available to them. Teachers also, not used to meeting students in this manner, need a period of adjustment. As with all significant change in learning programs, some faculty members welcome the new ideas and pursue with zest the added opportunities it offers them to bring the learning program much closer to the individual student. Many teachers comment that in a flexible schedule they are able to learn more about the students they work with faster than they could in all their previous years of teaching. Others find the adjustment of holding "appointments," seeing students individually and dealing with them in a tutorial relationship more difficult to adjust to.

It is during the students' and teachers' unstructured time (although structured for the teacher in that he makes himself available on a pre-arranged basis) that they meet in the area resource center. This available time permits the teacher to meet freely with students on individual problems. By meeting and talking privately with those students identified as having the greatest learning problems or seeking out special help, the teacher can now begin to meet the needs of his students.

Naturally it is not realistic to have a teacher meet as many as 150 students individually around the clock—but this is not necessary. At the high school level many students function well without needing individualized attention from *every* teacher. Therefore, the percentage of students who are reliant on extensive individual help is relatively small compared to the teacher load. With many students, just checking on their routine progress during individualized sessions does not take excessive amounts of time. During these brief sessions the instructor can make note of the problems that the learner has, his personal interests, areas of immediate concern and learning deficiencies. He can further make note of long range learning needs, including more extensive help for those who need it.

Laboratories

Certain departments in the school have facilities which tend to dominate the structure of the curriculum in that area. Home economics, industrial arts, science, business subjects are examples of curricula based on activity-centered learning. In these areas the laboratory serves as the area resource center and may be open a good part of the day to receive students. Open laboratories are a help to students who have to do catch-up work, either because they had difficulty in understanding the first time around or because they were out ill and missed some classes. They also permit a student interested in greater depth studies to explore and experiment beyond his normal classroom obligation. Indeed, the student's freedom to spend *all* his free mods, if he so chooses, in a departmental lab encourages potential vocational and avocational interests, a greater pursuit of excellence by the student in his field of interest, and a healthy testing of the student's use of free time in relationship to his other commitments.

In most cases laboratories are staffed by the teachers in that area. When possible, a trained department instructional para-professional or aide can be of great help. The amount of time a lab is open will, of course, depend on room space and utilization, the philosophy and acceptance of the open lab concept by the department as translated into a course configuration, and the overall staffing of the department. The Math Department might operate a lab staffed by unscheduled teachers where students would receive help or even give it to fellow students. The English, Social Studies and Science Departments could easily operate similar facilities. The Foreign Language Department could, in addition, provide a listening station where related tapes would be played. The amount and variety of this type of student work space is limited only by the imagination and the willingness of faculty members to develop them. Can students go to the typing rooms during free time either to do personal work or home work, or to catch up on class work? Can a stenography lab be developed similar to the language listening station? Can science classrooms and labs be open for make-up work or advanced work? Can the Industrial Arts Department open its doors to unstructured students who wish to continue work on their IA projects or make-up for lost time? May a student not enrolled in a course visit its large group session if he has an interest in the presentation and is unstructured at the right time? May a student invite himself to a single class meeting on the same basis? These are questions that only a faculty can answer. Their willingness to confront the variety of challenges each of these questions pose will to a large degree insure the success of the FMS program.

Guidance and administration

Student alternatives must also include appointments with the Guidance Office and Administration. Faculty, guidance and administration personnel must be willing to face an almost constant demand for their attention by an increasing number of students. Having a greater degree of free time, students will most certainly seek the services of people previously protected by the tight time factor.

Mini-courses

Most readers are familiar with the idea of a school offering mini-courses—non-credit, high interest, short duration courses. In a flexible schedule this becomes even more desirable and more possible. Teachers have greater motivation for initiating mini-courses because of their greater availability and freedom from repetitious acts. Mini-courses tend to reflect a particular interest on the part of the teacher as well as aim a special course at student interests. Courses taught by talented students could also be introduced. Titles such as jewelry crafts, dancing, languages, personal grooming, computer math, are just a small number of titles from an unlimited assortment that could be introduced. A mini-course needs only a teacher and a place to meet and you're set.

Other alternatives

There are a number of other options for student choice which should be mentioned. These include organizational meetings such as student council, school newspaper or service groups, which can meet on a regular or rotating schedule. The continuous availability of students makes the demands on guidance much greater, and increased time gives them an opportunity to deal with particular problems more immediately than in a traditional schedule. This is also true for the administration/student contact which increases significantly in a Flexible Modular Schedule. Many administrators will see a real advantage in this increased exposure to the students.

In this brief overview of possibilities it is easy to see that most schools could provide a rather impressive selection of student alternatives upon initiating an FMS program. Understandably this selection would become broader and better organized each year as both faculty and students work to come up with newer and better ideas to deal with student and faculty use of unstructured time.

Student accounting during unstructured time

If areas such as those outlined above are developed, it is essential to their success that students be permitted ready access to them while on their unstructured time. This means that a student does not need a pass to enter one of these facilities nor should he be required to sign up prior to his arrival. Either restriction limits the student's flexibility and ability to make decisions on the spot. It is understandable, where space factors limit the number of students permitted in one area, that a sign-up system may have to be used and adhered to.

It should also be noted that a flexible schedule allows the student to make decisions based on a short period of time, as students are forced to live with that decision only for the length of one mod. At the end of that mod they are free to make another decision on how to use their time. An example of how unstructured time may be used is presented here:

The student leaves his last morning class and is faced with a series of five free mods before his next scheduled class. He may choose to use his first two unstructured mods for lunch and head for the cafeteria. At the end of lunch he goes to the Guidance Office to look up a college catalog for one of the schools that interest him. While he is there he may or may not see his counselor. During the fourth and fifth unstructured mods he might go to the library for two mods of research. At the end of his last free mod he would head for his next structured class. During those five unstructured mods the school looses the ability to immediately contact the student. If it were necessary to locate the student, a number of spot checks at various places would probably result in his being found.

Structuring the problem student

In dealing with disciplinary infractions in a modern high school, detention, suspension, and even exclusion have their necessary roles to play. But now they need not be the automatic response to discipline that they once were; rather, an intermediate disciplinary system is established through the process of structuring.

Students who have difficulty making the right kind of decisions during their unstructured time usually surface early. In a flexibly scheduled school this student is less structured, and under these conditions he is more likely to make a series of wrong decisions about how he will use his unstructured time. In misusing his time the student becomes highly visible and is identified as a problem student. Once he is identified, the resources of the school can be mobilized to work with him in helping him understand some of his basic responsibilities.

The school should have a wide variety of resources which can be tailored to meet the specific needs of a single student in the case of a disciplinary infraction. The most obvious is that of taking away his unstructured time either by degree for varying lengths of time or totally if his behavior patterns are unacceptable. The student is then assigned (when not in class) to a structured study hall where attendance is taken and quiet enforced. Students can be structured in this way either by a teacher or as a result of administrative action.

Quite often a student will face up to his responsibility after one structuring experience. Other students need more time or different types of disciplinary experiences before they understand or are willing to accept personal responsibility for their own behavior.

Group counseling

The type of student mentioned above may very well be identified either by faculty, guidance or administration as having a need for counseling. Often, when the staff is available, group counseling sessions are productive. These counseling sessions are organized by the Guidance Department during the regular school day, with students assigned to a group which meets during a segment of their unstructured time—perhaps two to four mods each week. While guidance counselors guide and direct the sessions, it is important that the students be allowed to take an active role in the discussions. The group counseling sessions should serve not only as a means by which the student is told how the school views him and what changes will be necessary in his behavior but also as a way for the student to communicate to "the establishment" how he views it and what he finds difficult to deal with. In this way the group sessions provide a communications link between the school structure and the student and provide a means by which change may be effected, both within the student and within the organizational structure of the school. When it appears that the student has made the proper adjustment in his attitude or behavior he is allowed back into the mainstream during his unstructured time. It is just as important, however, that valid critical comments made by the students be followed up and acted upon by the school staff.

Disciplinary action for the disruptive student

If the student has been unable to make wise use of his unstructured time, it is important that the school help him by bringing some of its resources to bear. This might include scheduling regular conferences with his guidance counselor or a faculty member who can communicate well with him. Conferences with the school psychologist, guidance counselor, administrator, school nurse, coach or respected teachers should be scheduled as a necessary part of the students' program. Even outside agencies such as Mental Health Clinics, Child Welfare and Family Counseling Agencies may be called upon for help. Again, appointments can be made during the school day.

In dealing with disciplinary problems the parents of the problem student should not be neglected. Previously, parents could rely upon the traditional concept of the school role, based primarily on what school was like when they attended; in most instances the image would serve them well. In an FMS school, this is no longer possible. The whole structure of the school is new—and often incomprehensible—to parents. Misunderstanding can engender anger on the part of the parent, and a feeling that the organization of the school is at fault rather than his child's behavior. As a result the school becomes a greater target for people who are disenchanted with school. However, parents informed of the individual attention given by teachers to their son or daughter are usually appreciative of the school's interest and effort and often can gain a positive insight into the flexibility of the new schedule.

Meeting the needs of the academically faltering

In the case of academic difficulty related to a particular subject or subjects, the student can be handled in a number of ways. Since faculty members have greater amounts of free time than in a traditional schedule it is easier for them to set appointments for student-teacher conferences within the school day. If a student is having difficulty in chemistry, for example—a series of such conferences should be arranged for him with his chemistry teacher on their coinciding unstructured mods. Another alternative would be to assign the student to that department's lab area during a number of his unstructured mods each cycle. The student is expected to report to the lab on time the same way he would to a normally scheduled class. While in the lab he could make up work, receive special instruction from the teacher on duty or be tutored by a fellow student. A letter stating the reasons for this structuring and the anticipated outcomes should be sent to the parents to let them know how their child is functioning and how the school is attempting to help him. Still another way to cope with a student who has academic problems is to assign him more class time by structuring him to modules of another class in the same subject. It is even possible to schedule an entire class (or any part of it) for additional formal instruction. Once the students have mastered the requirement they can be released from the additional meeting.

Special attention is given to dealing with the academically faltering or the more disruptive student. Many schools are beset with the latter category of student but find it hard to control the entire school in order to cope with a few. It is suggested that the administration of a school would do better to try to control the five to ten percent of the students causing a disturbance than to impose restrictions on everyone. Also, greater exposure of the students who are generally weaker academic students will force the school to develop new alternative approaches to their education—a longstanding but rarely realized responsibility of the schools.

Summary

Chapter Seven deals with the heart of the issues of the program in a Flexible Modular Schedule. Few people complain about or criticize the reasoning behind the adaptation of a Flexible Modular Schedule. What concerns them is student performance during the unstructured time. Since a third of the student's day may be "free" time, the school must organize its resources to offer him constructive alternatives for the use of this time; otherwise the program could run into trouble. The role of the school Commons, where students can take a break during the school day, is discussed. Many schools offer a similar lounge or cafeteria arrangement; this idea of students "taking a break" is not unusual in schools today.

Other areas are needed in the school to accommodate the students for independent study time. The quiet study remains the traditional area for silent reading homework or other work. In an FMS school the Instructional Materials Center takes on new dimensions. Here most resources—learning materials, books, periodicals, audio-visuals, etc.—are housed for student use during out-of-class time. To supplement the IMC are area resource centers or laboratories for departmental use. Finally, school administration and guidance personnel are much more available to students because of the greater frequency of class-changing on the mod system and the larger amount of unstructured time.

A Strategy for Institutional Change

One requires no great insight to realize that the processes of improving schooling in the United States are haphazard if not chaotic. Millions of dollars are spent each year on consulting and a host of in-service education activities for teachers. But we seem no more capable of mounting a comprehensive change strategy than we were when all of this began. Worse, we know precious little about the change process in education and how we might go about accelerating it. Educational change, at even the most rudimentary levels, is one of those great unstudied realms of education. Obviously, understanding it is basic to effecting it. Need one have more motivation for probing into it?[1]

A Program for Planned Change

In this quote rests the crux of the problem facing the American High School today. Torn between the old authoritarian ways of the school administrators who could rule by fiat, and the more modern concept of "democratic leadership" (with the confusion that this implies) school administrators are faced with searching for a viable *strategy for change*. The modern school is a complex organization, based in a highly visable and volatile public arena. Assuming that an institutional objective such as flexible scheduling is not selected by

---

[1]Dr. John I. Goodlad, "Study and Effecting Educational Change," *I/D/E/A Reporter*, Fall Quarter, 1969, p. 3. "Institute for Development of Educational Activities, Inc., an Affiliate of the Charles F. Kettering Foundation."

the "authorities" and the teaching membership simply told to implement it (something which continues to happen), then a program for planned change must be designed and implemented. The most immediate question is also the most obvious: who should initiate the program of change and guide the organization to its goal of adopting the modular schedule? Someone in the organization must assume the responsibility for the implementation of a change strategy. Such a person is generally termed the change agent. It is not clear what the exact formula for success is in changing an institution, but some key elements can be analyzed to help guide the administrator or professional educator in the process. The remainder of the chapter is devoted to an explanation of the theoretical base or change model used in the Norwich program, followed by a more detailed description of the actual events which took place in the Norwich transition. The reason for the lengthy section devoted to the entire aspect of school change is that far too many administrators and other professional educators are not conversant with this aspect of their roles. The author is frequently asked, "What did you do in Norwich to bring this change about?" or, put another way, "Can you help tell me how to change a school?"

The analysis, although directed at introducing Flexible Modular Scheduling, may be used in implementing any organizational change.

Who Should the Change Agent Be?

All the literature points to the school principal as the key figure in producing the desired change in a school. Although studies have shown that everyone passes the buck when it comes to the failure to change—the superintendent blames the principal; the principal blames the superintendent; they both blame the teachers—it seems clear that the principal is a central figure in the change process. This is especially ironic when we are experiencing a sharp decline in that role's prestige, influence and concomitant power while at the same time the public and school critics are demanding an accelerated rate of change in the schools.

> We begin with the principal because any kind of system change puts him in the role of implementing the change in his school. I have never seen any proposal for system change that did not assume the presence of a principal in a school. I have yet to see in any of these proposals the slightest recognition of the possibility that the principal, by virtue of role, preparation, and tradition, may not be a good implementer of change.[2]

---

[2] Seymore B. Sarason, *The Culture of the School and the Problem of Change* (Boston: Allyn and Bacon, 1971), pp. 111-112.

It is imperative that the principal either initiate or help to facilitate the major changes in the school program. Other persons or groups are also influential, but without the support of the school principal the restructuring of the school as an institution is improbable. He must have extensive involvement and play an active leadership role, especially in a change such as FMS, since it is the building principal who is ultimately responsible for the construction of the school master schedule.

A change model

> Educational change today probably hangs up more on the lack of technical competence for implementation than it does on disagreement over what changes should take place.[3]

Although few courses dealing with organizational change are offered in college, there is a growing body of literature available in the areas of sociology and industrial psychology which deals with such change. Some of the work being done deals with change models or paradigms. One such model (Figure 8-1) will be used to demonstrate how an institution can be viewed in a change process.

The model's horizontal axis indicates the range and direction of change which can take place. The vertical column symbolizes the school. When the institution is in the middle, this represents the institution's theoretical state of equilibrium or the status quo.

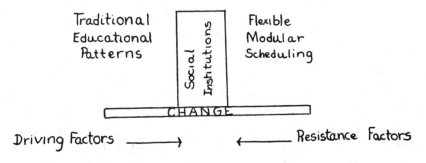

Figure 8-1

The inclusion of opposing forces, *driving factors* and *resistance factors*, sets the stage for our model. By identifying our educational objective, namely, Flexible Scheduling, we can fill in the specific countervailing forces which will present themselves in the dynamics of the change

---

[3]Allen and Bush, *A New Design For High School Education* (New York: McGraw-Hill, Inc., 1964.), p. vii.

(Figure 8-2). The institution moving to the right along the horizontal axis would indicate a successful strategy for change. If the institution moves to the left, this would indicate that the resistance factors have prevailed. Maintenance of the status quo would also reflect an unsuccessful attempt at change.[4]

Driving Factors	SCHOOL	Resistance Factors
Need for change		Community conservation—status quo
Student pressures		
Shortcomings of present program		Anti-administrative attitude
Meeting teacher needs		Philosophical
Administrative leadership		Fear of unknown
Philosophical		Method of decision-making
Professionalism		Fear of student reaction
Better use of teacher time		Resistance to new methods
New methodologies		Current student unrest
Additional district resources		Effect on academics
Faculty leadership		Effect on non-academic students
Reward system		Poor administrative leadership
		No reward system

Figure 8-2
Lining up the "Forces"

Resistance Factors

As a rule, it is advisable to first begin breaking down some of the resistance factors a faculty might have to the proposed change. This helps to create a more favorable setting for new ideas and alternate program designs. One way to do this is to look at your current schedule and detail its weaknesses or major blocking areas. At Norwich, the administration and the Guidance Department prepared a presentation for the faculty explaining the current problems with the traditional schedule. This led to the discussion of why we were considering another form of scheduling. The problems have been extensively detailed in Chapter Two and Three and will not be repeated here. It is enough to say that what might have seemed commonplace and obvious to those who had dealt with scheduling

---

[4] For a full analysis, consult *Planned Change*, by Ronald Lippit, Jeanne Watson and Bruce Westley (New York: Harcourt Brace Jovanovich, Inc., 1958).

was a new world to most of our teachers. Considerable time was spent in developing the faculty's understanding of schedule-making, because it was deemed important to share with them the intricacies and complexities of scheduling—both traditional and modular.

Naturally, teachers are more interested in program, and sufficient time should be devoted to the problems encountered in the scheduling of team teaching, teacher planning time, resource centers, mini-courses, etc., in the traditional schedule. This took place in Norwich at special faculty meetings where discussions were devoted exclusively to program considerations.

The faculty was also asked to read books such as *Individualized Learning Through Modular Flexible Scheduling* and *A New Design for High School Education* to help set into perspective the need for change in the educational system. There are also a number of anti-establishment books and movies[5] that are appropriate for use in helping to break down faculty resistance factors and leave faculty members more open to change.

Driving Factors

These are the forces that fill the vacuum created by the softening effect of the resistance factors. They must have an impact commensurate with the stage of faculty readiness, and, above all, be open and easily identifiable. Actually, Flexible Modular Scheduling is a better deal for faculty just as it will be a much better program for students. Teachers cannot be expected to change from what is tried and true unless the alternatives presented are clearly superior. Don't deal in abstracts or educational philosophy without meshing them with the practical aspects of what a new program "can do" for the individual teacher.

How Norwich Changed—An Analysis

The following analysis is based on the sequence of events that took place at Norwich during the change period. Some interpretation will be given but the reader should be able to recognize whether the activity was aimed at weakening resistance or whether it was a driving factor. The entire change process remains fluid and, on occasion, certain activities will serve the duel function of being both a driving factor and a resistance factor.

To begin a major program of faculty involvement in an organizational change such as FMS implies a period of temporary disequilibrium in the

---

[5] "The Improbable Form of Master Strum," from the Kettering Foundation.
"High School," by David Weisman.
"Questions and Answers," from the National Association of Secondary School Principals.

institution. The change agent must be able to deal with this with confidence and handle the transition with expertise if the change process is to be successfully negotiated.

Involving the Leadership

Since this analysis is based on the experiences of the author at Norwich Senior High School, it would be worthwhile to review some of the influences on the school personnel responsible for change at NSHS. I had been a student of Professor Deane Wiley, the co-author of the book *The Flexibly Scheduled High School,* at New York University. A broadening of my interest was attained when I attended an I/D/E/A-sponsored conference on school change at Amherst College in Massachusetts. This week-long program helped immensely by bringing together school leaders, many of whom were already experimenting or deeply involved with FMS.

After this experience I began to expose others in the high school administrative team to FMS. Robert Palmer, the Director of Guidance, and Paul Preuss, then the Assistant Principal and now Principal, both attended workshops and conferences on FMS sponsored by such groups as Educational Coordinates and the University of Massachusetts. To emphasize the growing interest in this program to both faculty and other concerned groups, and to more deeply confirm the feeling of involvement and commitment to the program, the Assistant Principal and the Director of Guidance visited Nova High School and Melbourne High School, both schools with a national reputation and both located in Florida.

After visiting these schools, noted for being model progressive institutions, the leadership became firm in their resolve to introduce this new program at Norwich and a strategy for change began to take shape.

Timing, a Key Factor

The initial task of the leadership team was to develop an overall timetable for the change process. Timing is especially important in the introduction of FMS to the faculty, because many educators have a negative attitude when they first encounter the new program. Unfortunately, the worst fears of many educators surface with the mention of FMS and emotionalism quickly takes an active role. The values of order, control, and traditional organization which have dominated our thinking for so many years are virtually redefined in FMS; this can be disconcerting to many people in the educational community. Fear of chaos, disorder, lack of pupil attendance and accountability, period by period, is engendered. Questions immediately asked are: "What's the matter with the old way?" "Don't you have more cutting?" "Who can remember where and when to go?" "How will you know where everyone is?" "Do we have the kind of kids that could be responsible enough to operate in this system?" "This is probably all right for the bright kids in suburban districts, but could our comprehensive group of students handle it?" The proposal will conjure up unnecessary but very human fears, the worst of which is: "Will we be sailing our ship—which we've always tried to keep on a steady keel—off the edge of the earth?"

So many people react with these initial feelings that it is necessary to program into your change timetable a reasonable reaction time lag. That is, from the initial introduction of the innovation to its formal study, enough time should elapse so that the faculty considering the change will no longer be emotionally charged but will be ready to research and investigate the new proposal on its merits.

Introducing the Study Phase

Although no formal pronouncements had been made to the faculty, the activity of the travelers, their reports back to the staff, faculty room conversations and other informal communications brought the terminology, "Flexible Modular Scheduling" to the fore. Although there was no more than mild curiosity on the part of a few of the more interested teachers, the stage has been set for introducing the subject to the faculty.

The formal introduction to the faculty of an educational study to consider the possibilities of FMS should be well planned. At Norwich, the introduction of the topic took place at an informational meeting in January. At this time the administration pointed out the mechanics of the new type of scheduling and some of its advantages. They proposed FMS as one idea to consider in relieving the scheduling blocks that we had encountered. It was an administrative alternative to satisfy the growing demands of the faculty for faculty planning time, teaching teams and more realistic time assignments—all of which had been requested. There was no need to be overly detailed; there would be plenty of time for that.

The groundwork was being laid. There are no areas of school life a teacher is more concerned about than his teaching schedule and the way he meets his students. Thus, the initial introduction of the topic FMS became an immediate interest to every staff member. Introducing the study phase a year and a half prior to the anticipated change left ample time to assess and adjust to the staff's attitudes. As expected, the meeting received a mixed reaction. Placing on the agenda basic topics such as scheduling and school reorganization implied a change in the wind—latent if not implicit. The idea of FMS was being introduced to a solid but generally conservative faculty. They had a good morale and a general feeling of satisfaction that Norwich was a fine school with good kids and a nice place to work. However, the initial reaction by a large segment of the faculty to FMS was one of being threatened. There was a strong feeling that FMS represented experimentation and that it was going to be forced on them.

The Committee

Ubiquitous in large corporations, municipalities, government agencies and schools is the *committee*. In this case, to carry on a comprehensive study of a topic as broad as FMS required a group of people particularly concerned about the topic. At the initial meeting with the faculty a request was made for interested persons to form a study committee. As expected, a number of people were willing to participate, and the committee soon totaled 16 in staff. By chance, most departments were represented; those which were not soon sent a representative. The school Principal, Assistant Principal, Director of Guidance, and Assistant Superintendent of Curriculum also joined the committee.

It is important for any committee to determine the task before it, and this was the subject of the first meeting. Is the committee's role to be educational and decision-making? What is the relationship of the committee to the rest of the faculty? How is the committee to proceed to gather information and how is this information to be disseminated? Will it be the committee that makes the final decision about whether the school adopts FMS, will it be the faculty, or will it be the administration? All of these questions were to be discussed by the committee in the weeks ahead.

Decision-making

It is best that the school leadership set some parameters prior to letting the study phase go to committee. At the first meeting the principal should identify who is to make the ultimate decision for moving to the new schedule and the part that various forces in the school community will play. Perhaps the superintendent and his team will play an important role, or maybe the principal will be permitted to make this a building level administrative decision. What role will the faculty be given in the decision-making process? If this is not clear prior to the first committee meeting, it will have to be resolved then or soon after. In any event, it should be assumed that the committee members will want to play a key role in determining the final decision. If the administration prefers not to leave the final decision in the hands of the committee, then this should be clearly understood by everyone.

Naturally, if the decision will be based only with the administration, then the role of the committee will be identified as purely educational. However, this approach—although simple—is discouraged by the author. It would be obvious immediately to any faculty member that his involvement would be only minimal. Since a change such as FMS will fundamentally restructure the school and have widespread ramifications for all of school life, it is strongly encouraged that both the committee and the entire faculty be given a strong voice in the decision-making. FMS requires genuine faculty support; the inculcation and acceptance of its principles and philosophy by the staff is essential. A goal of the change process should be to see that FMS and its basic tenants become a norm of the school's faculty. With this in mind, the Norwich leadership team decided that the faculty was to have the determining voice in whether they wanted FMS or not.

It was also determined from the beginning that the *modus operandi* of the investigation of FMS was to be *openness*. It was clear that the topic was controversial and needed lengthy debate. To oversell FMS would be a big mistake. These ideas were shared with committee members at the first meeting. Other than these limitations and guidelines, the committee was to function and determine its own course of action. A teacher was elected chairman at one of the first sessions. The group identified immediately that one of its roles was to educate themselves and the faculty on the rudiments of FMS. The committee was also to generate new ideas, gather additional information from other schools and, in general, become expert in the new scheduling. The first steps in the change process had been taken. Phase two was now to begin.

The Conflict

> Bringing about change in a school often creates high levels of conflict (conflict between principal and superordinates, between principal and teachers, between groups of teachers, between school and community). Initially, such a conflict is unavoidable and may even be desirable. Ultimately, the management of such a conflict is crucial to a successful change.[6]

Central to any theme of change is the social and institutional phenomenon of conflict. This, it should be pointed out, is not necessarily an undesirable state of the organization. Quite the contrary. Many writers point out that a certain amount of tension is productive. It would be unrealistic to think that a change of any magnitude, especially one such as

---

[6]Goodlad, I/D/E/A Reporter, p. 9.

FMS, will not meet differing degrees of both acceptance and rejection. The nature of this issue makes it unavoidable to dodge the pending schism. Thus, the strategy developed to handle change must be able to confront the hurdles of controversy.

The emotional resistance to FMS

In other chapters we dealt with the practical and philosophical reasons for moving to a new type of schedule. Now it would be worthwhile to review the central reasons why FMS stirs such strong—often emotional—resistance among its adversaries.

Concern for student and youth behavior has become a major preoccupation with most Americans. In general, there are two camps of thought revolving around the current problems of school. One says that the problems today are the result of the corruption of youth by the Dewey-Spock-Progressive group resulting in an overly permissive attitude taken by parents and schools. The other school of thought feels that the school curriculum and structure is overly restrictive, blocking the individual's creative development. There is a surfeit of writers taking this second point of view who claim the schools are a "wasteland," that they stifle self-expression, etc.

The more conservative camp would interpret the greater emphasis on student self-reliance and freedom of choice in FMS as a continuing undesirable trend in secondary schools towards further liberalization. The proposed change to FMS will serve to stir their strong feelings and engender a sincere desire to make a stand on such an obvious and far-reaching change. Other changes in the school program are often less visible to public view, or they are so sophisticated that the average layman does not comprehend them. This leaves some changes to become the symbols of resistance. The introduction of sex education is such an example. The change from the traditional to the modular schedule may also be such a sign. Naturally, the degree of resistance from both the faculty or community will vary depending on many factors, including the all-important educational and informational phase to be carried out with both the school professionals and the public.

At Norwich it was now time to move ahead. The stage had been set, the players identified. The controversy that was to sweep the building became focused in the FMS Committee and the next few months were to be a trying but exciting period of activity.

Organizing the Conflict

The leadership team had thought through several major aspects of the planned program of change. It was determined that the latest a final decision could be reached as to whether or not we adopted FMS was January. After that date, arrangements for developing departmental and course configurations would have to be made and the master schedule constructed.

A most important point was the method by which the issue was to be resolved. It was felt that the decision was too important to be determined by the committee alone, thus it was decided to bring the issue of FMS to a full faculty vote. This would meet the requirements for the ultimate involvement of the faculty in the decision-making process. It would further serve to resolve the conflict between factions in the faculty far better than having the change imposed. It seemed to be the only acceptable resolution open.

School Visits

The FMS Committee decided that the best way to expose its members as well as other faculty to FMS was to have each visit a number of schools in our geographic area. It was arranged that faculty members going on the trips would leave after the completion of school, travel to their destination, and stay overnight. The next day committee members would spend the full time visiting a FMS school, returning home that night. Unfortunately, at that time we had to travel a considerable distance to find another FMS school.[7] Today there are many more accessible schools in an area than there were in 1969.

Six faculty members went on each trip to visit a school already on FMS. Although many were overnight trips, several schools were located in the general area, permitting day trips for those who preferred not to be away overnight. No trip exceeded $100 in expense, and colleagues covered classes in each department. This kind of cooperation helped avoid excessive substitutions.

These trips proved to be highly successful. Besides the wide exposure to other schools, an unexpected secondary benefit resulted. Since the rides

---

[7]Schools visited by members of the faculty included:
Abington North Campus, Abington, Pa.
Timberlaine Regional High School, Planstow, N.H.
Alexis I. DuPont High School, Wilmington, Del.
Greece Arcadia and Olympia High School, Greece, N.Y.
Bishop Grimes High School, Syracuse, N.Y.
North Haven, Conn.
Bethlehem Central, Albany Area (not FMS)
Nova High School, Fl.
Melbourne High School, Fl.
Oceana Senior High School, Pacifica, Calif.
J.K. Kennedy Senior High School, Fremont, Calif.
Serramonte High School, Daly City, Calif.
Mission San Jose Senior High School, Fremont, Calif.

were long, the members had time to exchange views and talk through their respective ideas and feelings about the proposed school changes. An intimacy and trust developed among the staff that ordinarily could not have taken place during the normal school working day. The faculty was eager to participate on these trips even though they received no extra compensation. We were all engaged in a true educational experience and the investment in time by each person was a willing contribution.

Each group that visited a school (and there was only one teacher who refused to go) reviewed their experience when they returned and issued a written report to all faculty members about the trip. Pros and cons of the school program visited were described, along with a statement about its implications for Norwich. Later all this information was pulled together at a special faculty meeting.

Involving Outside Faculty

While visits were taking place, the committee reviewed and approved the idea of inviting several faculty members from an out-of-state school to visit Norwich and spend the day. Luck had it that six staff members from North Haven High School, North Haven, Connecticut, a school which had been on a mod schedule for a number of years, were permitted to come to Norwich on a conference day. Norwich, of course, paid mileage, motel and meals. The North Haven team consisted of an Assistant Principal, the Director of Guidance, and four department chairmen—math, science, social studies, and English. After a general session at Norwich in which the North Haven program was outlined, the entire Norwich staff divided into six groups. This gave the Norwich faculty the opportunity to quiz thoroughly people actively involved in an FMS program. This interaction went a long way to assuaging many faculty fears and helped deal with the nitty gritty questions of *who, how, what, when,* and *under what circumstances.* Total cost of the in-service session was less than $150, and it was a fantastic success.

A Consultant Handles Some Road Blocks

As the faculty was actively engaged in its pursuit of knowledge about FMS, it was felt by the administration that it would be helpful if an outside, neutral person came in to assess the change program and the faculty's readiness for innovation.[8] Dr. Arthur Blumberg, a psychologist with extensive experience in school and industrial bureaucracies and a member of the Syracuse Department of Educational Administration, was

---

[8]Alexander M. Swaab, "Organizational Change and the Principal," ORGANIZATIONAL CHANGE IN THE SCHOOLS; *Educational Technology* Oct. 1972, pp. 55-57.

invited in to do the job. He spent two days with the faculty, interviewing everyone in small groups of six to eight people. He also spent time with the administration staff in the Superintendent's office and at the building level.

The result of his activities was positive. The consultant identified that, in general, the faculty was favorably inclined and willing to go along with the change. He did point out a number of problems which, if resolved quickly, would go a long way toward reducing tensions and firming up faculty support. For example, he pointed out that although the committee had decided on a faculty vote, no date had yet been set. This led to questions as to whether there was really going to be a vote and, if so, would it take a simple majority to pass it or would there have to be a significant percentage of favorable responses. Both these questions had widespread implications. After the consultant's visitation, the next committee meeting was devoted to dealing with his findings. The meeting attempted to generate some answers to the above-mentioned blocking points.

The consultant's visit proved to be invaluable. Although a change process appears to be based on common sense—and indeed it is—sometimes its participants are so close to what is happening that the simple, obvious problems are frequently overlooked. Often these are more important to deal with than the big splash of a school visit, in-service program, etc. Although the change to FMS might well have taken place without this extra help, the consultant played a major role in facilitating the faculty's transition through the change process.

Public Relations

Throughout the entire "campaign" there should be an active public relations program. This includes news coverage through school-generated news releases, radio shows, and presentations to public groups and clubs. The coordinator of this program should be the change agent himself so that the activities of the school committees, field trips and conferences get full public exposure.

If a serious error was made in the Norwich change strategy it was that there was not enough public information and communication with parents prior to the faculty vote. There were the standard releases, but unfortunately few people in the community give this information much heed until a controversy erupts. Had more community citizens been involved we might have had greater initial acceptance of the program. As it was, the decision was made to let the faculty, as professionals, actively debate and decide the issue on its merits without any undue influence from outside sources. It was then our intent to "sell" the program to the lay public.

This almost worked. A dissident staff member went to the press with a series of unsigned letters criticizing the program as too experimental and progressive. Although this type of criticism is to be expected, a good positive public relations program and active community involvement can head off a lot of headaches.

Part of this public relations program is the need to inform the local board of education of the merits of the new program and the faculty's activities. Board members can serve as excellent communicators with the community served by the school, and they certainly should be appraised of the new program.

Final review and vote

After a hectic three months of school visits, outside resource people and continuous dialogue, the FMS committee (or Mod Squad as it became known) organized a final review meeting for the faculty. Members of each visiting committee were put on a panel, as were members of the FMS committee. At this meeting each faculty member making the presentation was to evaluate the visit and present his own conclusions. Also, a date for the final vote was set, as was the procedure for voting—one for each faculty member with no distinctions made for part-time, full-time, respective teaching, support or administration positions.

A serious question arose over whether the vote should be all or nothing for the ensuing school year. A minority felt that an option should be a vote in favor of FMS " . . . but let's wait another year or longer." This was a showdown committee vote and it was decided to present the proposal stipulating that, if passed, it would take effect the following year. If someone was indeed in favor of FMS but felt that we were moving too fast, he would vote "no" on the proposal. In the event the proposition was defeated, the vote could be analyzed later for reasons for the defeat. It was also established that a 65 percent favorable vote would be the minimum acceptable. Any smaller margin might divide the faculty too much.

On January 8, 1970, immediately following the Christmas vacation, the faculty voted. The final tally was 78 percent pro (46 votes) and 22 percent against (12 votes). Flexible Modular Scheduling had been approved by the faculty.

Summary

Proposing a major change in an educational institution is no easy task. The change agent, identified in this chapter as the building principal, must have some expertise in bringing about change, handling conflict and involving the organizational membership. Norwich experienced such a change when moving from a traditional schedule to one of the first high schools in New York State to adopt a Flexible Modular Schedule. A year and a half was devoted to dealing with the transition. Using Lippett's model, resistance factors and driving factors are viewed in relation to the change model used in the discussion.

A committee was formed to help guide the study phase of the change. Through the committee, trips were taken to other schools, outside faculty visited Norwich to discuss with out staff the intricacies of FMS, special meetings were held to discuss scheduling and program, and an outside consultant helped clear away some of the communications hurdles.

In order for each participant to have the maximum impact on the decision-making, a date was set on which each faculty member, whether administrator or aide, would get one vote. In this way the faculty by a 78 to 22 percent margin voted in favor of Flexible Modular Scheduling.

9

Evaluating the Program in a
Flexible Modular Schedule

Educators who are exposed to flexible scheduling for the first time often ask if research studies have concluded that it is better than a traditional schedule. The answer, of course, is no. Research has not judged a flexible schedule better than a traditional schedule. Similarly no research study has or can answer the question of whether a fifty-minute period is better than a forty-minute period. The schedule a school uses is only one factor—only one variable—in any significant evaluation of a school program.[1]

Evaluating a schedule

The above statement accurately poses a major dilemma for all forms of education. Do we have the necessary tools to accurately test an educational program of any sort—carefully screening out and identifying the host of independent variables that can change behavioral outcomes in testing? As we become more sophisticated about our objectives in education, including not only the cognitive domain but also such areas as critical thinking, creativity, independent initiative, constructive use of free time and greater conceptual development, we are entering into a new realm for the school—one we have not been success-

---

[1] Donald C. Manlove and David W. Beggs, III, *Flexible Scheduling: Bold New Venture* (Bloomington: Indiana University Press, 1965), p. 184.

fully able to test. The latter falls squarely in the affective behavioral area of learning.

It is interesting to note that a change such as flexible scheduling in a school often brings forth loud cries for extensive evaluation—this in communities where evaluation probably never before existed or was completely taken for granted. No one researches the effects of the differences between a school day that runs from 8:00 a.m. to 3:00 p.m. rather than 9:00 a.m. to 2:00 p.m., or the impact on student learning of schools that go to double and even triple sessions. How much information exists in research studies to guide communities or school administrators in determining whether courses should be 40, 50, or 60 minutes in length in a traditional schedule? Even such a fundamental and important question as the value of homogeneous versus heterogeneous groupings in schools is still to be decided by the educational researchers. How then can anyone effectively mobilize enough data to make conclusive claims about one type of schedule versus another? Especially when it has been the underlying tenet of this book that the flexible schedule is only a vehicle that the administrator and faculty can use to increase the school's number of program elections. How and to what degree these program options will be exercised and the effect of any one of them on the learning situation is indeed difficult to isolate. However, the fact that it may be difficult does not absolve the educational community from having to address itself to this responsibility. It would be unfortunate if, at this juncture, undue or unreasonable demands for "proof" to satisfy a hostile community were required of the planned change.

The available data

The foregoing discussion does not mean to imply that there is no collecting of data or ongoing evaluation of flexible scheduling taking place in schools. On the contrary, schools moving into the new system have often been forced—out of necessity—to do a much more extensive evaluation of their program than ever before. The net result of this is a growing body of empirical data that strongly supports the programs in schools that have adopted a Flexible Modular Schedule. So affirmative is the data, in fact, that communities interested in school evaluations might well ask themselves why they continue to operate their schools in a traditional pattern.

For the reader's interest and analysis, the data will be presented in two parts. The first is a general review of the available literature, including other studies in the field. The second part will be an analysis of the Norwich Senior High School program in its first year of operation under a flexible schedule in comparison to the three previous years before its inception.

A review of the literature

It would be difficult to evaluate any program unless there were some stated objectives which differentiate the Flexible Modular Schedule from other programs. Dr. David Beggs of Indiana University, who has done considerable work in the area of flexible scheduling, offers these specific objectives:[2]

1. To improve instruction.
2. To use teaching talent more effectively.
3. To provide students with the opportunity to study independently.
4. To provide a practical means of individualizing instruction.
5. To conserve teacher time.
6. To provide better-sized learning groups.
7. To provide better use of facilities.

Dr. Maxey, in a series of studies carried out in three separate school districts using FMS (Fresno Unified District of California, LaDue High School in Missouri and Delevan-Davern High School in Delevan, Wisconsin), made the following conclusions about techniques to be used in evaluating FMS:[3]

1. Observable behavior can be evaluated by recording patterns of classroom activity.
2. Student, teacher, and parental views of FMS can be assessed via opinionaires.
3. Relative effectiveness of IS, LG, and SG activity can be evaluated through the use of opinionaires.
4. Teaching effectiveness can be determined through comparative achievement testing.

Although there have been a number of studies completed as of this writing, the limitations of space prohibit an extensive review of all the material. Instead, only some of the more important studies will be reviewed. The interested reader may refer to the government ERIC files,

---

[2]Dr. James Maxey, "Evaluation of the Outcomes of Modular Scheduling," The Iowa Center for Research in School Administration, University of Iowa, Dec. 1968, p. 2. ERIC ED 026 733.

[3]Maxey, "Evaluation," p. 8.

sponsored by the U.S. Department of Health, Education and Welfare, Office of Education, for a copy of most of the studies done to date.

Speckhard studies

The move to FMS by the first schools took place in the 1963-64 school year. Since then there have been a number of broad research studies done to verify or support major claims by proponents of FMS. The most authoritative of these were carried out by Dr. Gerald Speckhard of Valparaiso University. Two Colorado high schools, both in the same district, were compared first in 1965 and again in 1968. One school was on a modular schedule and the other a traditional schedule. A summary of Dr. Speckhard's findings from studies in 1964 and again in 1968 show that on Stanford Achievement Tests "the students at a modularly scheduled high school perform as well or better than students in a school with a traditional schedule."[4]

A number of questionnaires and educational tests were administered both to students and to faculty. These were analyzed in an attempt to (1) test the basic theoretical claims made by advocates of modular scheduling, and (2) test whether or not there would be any change over a longitudinal period in the experimental school.

One of the questionnaires administered to the pupils was a "My High School" opinionnaire. The items on the questionnaire were developed to assess the opinions and attitudes toward three aspects of high school education: (a) opinions about the school program in general, (b) opinions about teachers and teaching practices, and (c) opinions about student responsibility for education and enjoyment of going to school. A summary of the results shows that the students from the experimental school which was flexibly scheduled reported more positive opinions on 17 of the 25 questions asked. On the remaining eight items there was no significant difference.

On the three questions that reflected opinions about a student's responsibility for his own education and enjoyment of school, the students from the flexibly scheduled school scored significantly higher. Speckhard also reports that "for the ten items reflecting student attitudes toward the school program in general, the students at the experimental school scored higher on all items but one."[5] He goes on to say:

> Thus it can be concluded from the My High School opinionnaire that the students at the experimental school have more positive opinions about

---

[4]Gerald Speckhard, "An Evaluation of the Educational Program of a High School Using a Modular Schedule, a Follow-up Study," ERIC Document EDO25840, Sept. 1968, p. 33.

[5]Speckhard, "An Evaluation," p. 29.

their high school education, but these positive opinions are related more to the school program in general and student responsibility for education than to teaching and teaching practices.

Speckhard also worked with standardized achievement tests. These, which included the Tests of Educational Development (ITED), the Brown-Holtzman Survey of Study Habits and Attitudes, and the Watson-Glazer Critical Thinking Appraisal, were administered to the seniors at both high schools. Because of their importance, his findings are presented at length from the original study:
The results show:

> There is no significant difference between the two schools or inter-actions with treatment effects for the following subtests in the ITED battery:

> 1. Understanding of Basic Social Concepts
> 2. Background in the Natural Sciences
> 4. Ability to Do Quantitative Thinking
> 6. Interpretation: Natural Sciences
> 7. Interpretation: Literature
> 8. General Vocabulary

Significant differences in treatment effects and/or interactions were found for the following tests:

Correctness and Appropriateness of Expression. (3) The students at the modular high school scored significantly higher than the control high school on the measure of correctness and appropriateness of expression. This result is consistent over the three ability groups but not for both sexes. The girls at the modular scheduled high school scored very significantly higher than the girls at the control school, but the boys at the two schools did not differ significantly from each other.

Interpretation: Social Studies. (5) The students at the modularly scheduled high school performed very significantly higher than the students at the control high school on the ability to interpret social studies materials. This result is consistent over the three ability groups and for both sexes.

Use of Sources of Information. (9) The students at the modularly scheduled high school performed very significantly higher than the students at the control high school on the measure of use of sources of information. This finding is consistent over the three ability levels and for both sexes.

Watson-Glaser Critical Thinking Appraisal. No significant difference was found between the two schools in critical thinking ability. This finding is consistent over the three ability groups and for both sexes.

Brown-Holtzman Survey of Study Habits and Attitudes. No significant difference was found between the two schools for the students' reports of their study habits and attitudes. This finding is consistent over the three ability groups and for both sexes.

A summary of the Iowa Test results, 1965 and 1968, show that the two evaluations "generally indicate that the modularly scheduled school is equal to or better than the control high school in academic achievement. The Watson-Glaser Critical Thinking Appraisal in the 1965 study showed the experimental school to be superior in critical thinking, but this was not confirmed by the later test. In the Brown-Holtzman Survey of Study Habits and Attitudes, the test was consistent for the two studies and did not show any significant differences between the two schools."

Speckhard's general conclusions are presented to the reader at length:

> Although the practices at Broomfield High School during 1968 were somewhat more consistent with theory than was disclosed in the 1965 study, the students and teachers still do not fully use, or possibly understand, some of the opportunities for improving the educational program which are made possible with a modular system.
>
> The use of large group sessions for discussion or for individual study, though not used frequently at Broomfield, appears to be practiced more often than is consistent with theory. Large group sessions should be used almost solely for presentation. Discussion, according to theory, should be reserved for small group sections where wide participation and discussion in depth can take place. The use of small group sections for study purposes, while not practiced widely, was reported to occur often enough to suggest that small group practices also are not completely consistent with the theory of the modular system. The most effective practices for small group sections are pupil-teacher interaction, pupil-pupil interaction, group projects, and analytical and exploratory discussion. Individual study, of course, should be reserved for supervised or unsupervised study time.
>
> In spite of the shortcomings noted above, the reported practices at Broomfield High School are generally in agreement with the theory of the modular system. The 1968 results, while similar to the findings in 1965, indicate a slight trend toward greater consistency with expected practices.
>
> While the reported problems remain similar to those disclosed in 1965, the current evaluation found that low ability students reported their problems to be of a lesser degree than was reported in 1965. This suggests that some improvement has been made in making the program work for low ability students. Very few problems were found to be of a greater degree in 1968 than in 1965, and a number of problems were reported to be of a slightly lesser degree. This indicates a trend toward improvement in the use of the modular system at Broomfield.

As in 1965, both the students and the teachers have strong favorable attitudes toward the school program. Additional support for the modular system was provided by the more favorable opinions of the school program, as measured by the My High School opinionnaire, in comparison to the control school.

The test results disclosed that the students at the modularly scheduled high school perform as well or better than students in a school with a traditional schedule. However, the superiority in critical thinking, disclosed in 1965, was not maintained in 1968.

The conclusions can be summed up by saying that Broomfield's program, generally good in 1965, has maintained about the same level of quality with slight improvements in certain areas of the modular system. The opinions of the school program are highly favorable, and growth in academic achievement is equal to or greater than the achievement at a relatively comparable control school in the same school district.[6]

Headcount study

Still another study was done at Delevan-Darian High School in Wisconsin to check out the use by students of their unassigned time. A shadow study was designed to gather observable data about student use of their unassigned time. Also, a headcount was designed to assess the amount of unscheduled time available to students and the way they were using this time. During the study the number of students that frequented the open labs, student lounge, cafeteria, etc., was tabulated, as well as the number of modules of time during the instructional cycle the student was scheduled. In this program, 60.5 percent of the student's time was scheduled and 39.5 percent of his time was unscheduled.

The findings of the headcount survey revealed that 77 percent of the students' unscheduled time was engaged in learning activities with only 23 percent of the students' free time spent in the Commons areas.[7]

In the shadow study, a random selection of students was shadowed by trained observers. Eighty-one students were shadowed one complete school day. An effort was made to get equal representation from each grade level and from varying ability levels. The study indicated that most students used their free time well. However, as might be expected, some lower ability students displayed a lack of responsibility during this time by frequenting the student lounge and cafeteria too often. School administrators knowing this can prepare procedural revisions in the program aimed at balancing the program for certain individuals.

---

[6]Speckhard, "An Evaluation," pp. 32-33.

[7]"The Evaluation Study of the Delevan-Darian High School New Design Instructional Program," Delevan-Darien High School, Delevan, Wisconsin, 1968.

Abington study

In another study, done at Abington High School in Pennsylvania, entitled "An Analysis of the Relationship of Scheduled Class Time and Achievement Under Two Methods of Instruction," the author, Anastasia M. Hagan, although identifying the limited nature of the test, concludes:

> The analysis of covariance and an examination of the mean change in achievement for each group direct that achievement may be inversely related to the amount of scheduled class time. . . . Such a relationship seems to indicate that where a small amount of class time forces the student to use a significant amount of his own time for learning, he achieves more than he would in a situation where most of the learning takes place during time which is scheduled for him. It also proposes that on his own time, the student is a more active learner and thus achieves more. The value of this result, then, lies in a proposal for further study of a flexible time plan and the continued development and use of independent study time within a high school program. There are positive indications that a student's success in studying a structured subject may be aided by a program which incorporates class time and independent study time.[8]

This study, carried on in the math program at Abington High School North Campus under Title III, had the purpose of comparing the achievement and attitudes of ninth-grade algebra students who used programmed texts with those of students who used conventional texts when the students were given a choice of varying degrees of contact with the teacher.

A lengthy pupil-opinion poll was taken at Northeast High School, a large high school of 2,000 pupils in St. Petersburg, Florida. This evaluation report is reproduced in its entirety in the Appendix.

A composite of the studies

Although there are other studies that have been completed, those included in this report represent some of the more representative ones. In general, the research to date has been summarized by Dr. Hansen in a Measurement Research Corporation monograph presented below:[9]

> 1. Students are sold. A large majority of students who have been involved in both flexible and conventional programs prefer the

---

[8] Anastasia M. Hagan, "An Analysis of the Relationships of Scheduled Class Time and Achievement Under Two Methods of Instruction." Abington North Campus: ERIC Paper. EA002323/ED030203.

[9] Burdette P. Hansen, Ph.D.; "Evaluation of Flexible Modular Scheduling," Measurement Research Cooporation Monograph extract; Vol. VI, February, 1969.

flexible. And students in flexible schools most frequently state that flexibility and self-responsibility are the things they like most about their school. On the other hand, students in conventional schools most frequently criticize the regimentation on open-ended questions.

2. Students under independent and self-directive study plans make much greater use of resource materials and special facilities than they do under a conventional program.

3. Students in flexible programs score significantly higher than students in traditional classes on tests of critical thinking.

4. On standardized achievement tests, such as the I.T.E.D., there are no systematic differences between mean scores by students in flexible and traditional schools.

5. However, teachers rate student achievement higher for students under independent study than for students under conventional class instruction.

6. Teachers in flexible and conventional schools rate student behavior about the same. This is true also on "before" and "after" ratings by teachers who have been involved in a change-over.

7. Teachers involved in the transition from conventional to modular vote to continue with the modular after one year or more of experience in a large majority of schools that have changed. Also, teachers in schools with both types of classes rate the flexible program higher than the conventional.

8. Teachers and students consistently rate independent study and small group instruction higher than large group instruction.

9. Teachers report that they have and use more time in preparation under a flexible program than under a conventional one. However, this is reported as one of the problem areas by teachers in flexible programs, with teachers indicating that they believe they do not use unscheduled time as constructively as they should.

10. Teachers believe that they put in longer hours and their work load is heavier under a flexible program than under a traditional program. However, classroom hours and student loads are no greater, and often are lighter.

11. Studies on teacher morale in flexible and traditional schools show no important differences.

Norwich program objectives met

Sometimes it is easier for the school administrator or other professional personnel to analyze a specific case of a school in the process of change and the effects on the school of the adoption of a new program. It is for this reason that the example of Norwich Senior High School is used. Actually Norwich presents a good working model. The school, which has 800 students comprising grades 10 to 12, offers a comprehensive educational program. About a third of its graduates go on to four-year colleges, another third participate in some form of continuing education, and approximately one-third are terminal. The school is located in a conservative community with few pressures to change or liberalize its program.

The Norwich faculty generally reflected community attitudes and were traditional in their outlook. They were also willing to try new ideas, given the proper opportunity. Flexible scheduling was adopted by this faculty primarily because it offered them the chance to implement the design features of the Trump Plan. These objectives included the restructuring of program and personnel to include team teaching, variable class meeting patterns, independent study, and individualized instruction.

Team teaching

> Team teaching enables teachers to confer during the school day, to question each other about the best way to present a particular unit, to utilize each other's strengths, to expose more students than a teacher's own 100-125 to a particular teacher especially talented in some area of a course. Team teaching provides intellectual stimulation for both faculty and students.[10]

Prior to moving to the flexible schedule three teaching teams operated at Norwich, two in social studies and one in chemistry. Two of these had planning time built into the schedule. There had been a number of other requests for teaming from time to time but schedule limitations prohibited their functioning. In moving to the new schedule it was our specific objective to permit teams of teachers to create new programs utilizing and relying on team-teaching techniques, both intra-departmental and interdisciplinary. This was achieved by teacher initiative, and voluntary requests for teams were satisfied in the following areas:

10th Mixed—English-Social Studies (Non-Academic)

11th Core—English-Social Studies (Non-Academic)

10th Academic Social Studies

10th Academic English

11th Academic Social Studies

---

[10]"What Is Modular Scheduling?", Annual Report, 1967, of the Evanston Township High School (mimeographed).

11th Academic English

12th Academic English

12th (Non-Academic) English

Chemistry

Consumer Economics (Non-Academic)

Ninth Grade Math

Tenth Grade Math

Eleventh Grade Math

Significantly, planning time for each team was built right into the schedule.

Independent Study and Use of Unstructured Time

Charles Silberman, in his classic study *Crisis in the Classroom,* summarizes an element he found common in most schools:

> The most important characteristic schools share in common is a preoccupation with order and control. . . . One of the most important controls is the clock . . . school is a place where things happen not because students want them to, but because it is time for them to occur. This in turn means that a major part of a teacher's role is to serve as traffic manager and timekeeper, either deciding on a schedule himself or making sure that a schedule others have made is adhered to.[11]

The success or failure of the independent study phase of a high school program is particularly difficult to evaluate. There are of course great numbers of students who are responsible and who use their time efficiently and effectively. Often it is easy to forget about this "silent majority" who actively go about getting the job done. For them the additional unstructured time is very important, and day-in and day-out they make good use of this time. However, each school has a small percentage of students who are not mature enough to make effective use of their time. These students spend most of their unassigned time in the Commons. In an attempt to analyze the way in which students at Norwich were generally using the Commons, a cursory headcount was taken. Students who were doing school work, reading or engaged in recognizably related activities were counted as "number working." (See Figure 9-1).

---

[11]Silberman, *Crisis in the Classroom:* pp. 123-124.

COMMONS SURVEY

Date	Day & Mod	No. in Commons	No. Working	Percentage
Nov. 13	F/14	98	44	45%
19	D/1	66	60	90%
20	E/2	48	20	42%
30	B/3	85	48	57%
Dec. 1	C/2	122	73	59%
1	C/15	69	33	48%
1	C/16	140	50	36%
2	D/15	65	35	54%
2	D/16	82	44	53%
3	E/5	142	50	35%
9	C/6	79	22	28%
10	D/4	58	27	46%
10	D/5	68	14	21%
10	D/7	108	30	28%
16	B/4	100	31	31%
Jan. 18	D/5	73	29	40%
18	D/6	78	36	46%
Mar. 25	D/2	71	45	63%
25	D/3	55	29	53%
TOTAL		1607	720	44%

Figure 9-1

This survey points out two distinct but understandable phenomena. One is that a far larger percentage of students use Commons to work in than one would suspect. This can be interpreted to mean that many students (a) can work with noise, (b) prefer the informality of group work sessions for such things as math problem-solving, stenographic studies, etc., (c) enjoy working and having a snack. A second trend seems to be that there is a greater concentration of students studying earlier in the morning than later in the day. That is, as the day wears on there is less interest or reason for a student to use his time studying.

This study, along with the earlier shadowing study at Delevan, would confirm the fact that a large percentage of the students tend to use their Independent Study time effectively, including some students, who are thought to use too much of their free time to go to Commons. This in spite of the fact that many teachers and lay people alike make the assumption that all students seen in Commons are automatically wasting their time.

Absenteeism and tardiness

> Student absenteeism and tardiness have been on the rise the past five years, reversing a previous trend towards better attendance. The new trend is costly in terms of lost learning opportunity and unused facilities, state educators note.[12]

The statewide average for daily attendance was 93 percent of pupils in school, down from 94.5 percent in 1963-64, seven years earlier. Cities have the poorest averages, with district superintendencies slightly worse off than village areas.

> The reasons for absenteeism are local strife, suburban affluence and city problems and distractions such as crime, poverty and the transient nature of the population, noted Henry R. Kunze, associate in school attendance in the Education Department. He also lists neglect or privation at home, marital discord, overprotection of parents, and physical or social pathology. Kids stay home because they're unhappy with the curriculum, don't want to take gym, or the parents work and don't make the kids go to school.[13]

If flexible scheduling represents any advantage for the student which makes school a better, more humane place to come to, this should reflect itself in the attendance figures. The attendance at Norwich in comparison to other years was very favorable, as the figures will show. As with all such statistics other variables came into play. The nurse's position at the high school was increased from a part-time to a full-time position. Since she played an active role in pupil attendance her presence had some influence. Nevertheless the attendance data did prove to be impressive.

In each of the first five months, the school exceeded previous attendance marks for the *prior three years*.

In all, six of the ten months of the school calendar showed the highest percentage attendance for the time measured. What's more, the increase in January took place during an unusually severe winter. (See Figure 9-2).

Dropout rate

The dropout rate tends to be a volatile barometer of the acceptance of a program in that it tends heavily to reflect prevailing economic condi-

[12]"Problems in the High Schools," *Inside Education*, Publication of the N.Y.S. Education Department, June 1961, pp. 4-7.

[13]"Problems," *Inside Education*, p. 5.

NORWICH SENIOR HIGH SCHOOL MONTHLY ATTENDANCE RECORD

	Sept.	Oct.	Nov.	Dec.	Jan.	Feb.	March	Apr.	May	June	Yr.
1967 1968	97	95.1	93.7	93	90.6	94.4	94.2	93.6	93.9	96.3	94.2
1968 1969	95.5	94.3	91.5	90	91.7	93.1	93.2	94.1	96.0	98.4	93.8
1969 1970	95.3	94.1	93.3	93.9	91.8	93.8	93.8	96.4	92.7	97.7	94.25
1970 1971	97.6	95.84	94.17	94.53	94.30	90.6	95.4	94.4	94.8	96.2	95.2
%Gain Over Next Highest Year	+.6	+.7	+.4	+.6	+2.5		+1.2				Higher than Previous Years

Figure 9-2

tions in the community. Other things such as the vocational school and program developments also are factors. Pregnancies are not counted. The first year in the mod schedule at Norwich reduced the dropout rate to the lowest rate in four years based on final enrollment (June). The figures for the four years are:

Year	%
1968	4%
1969	3.5%
1970	5%
1971	3%

Achievement testing—Regents

In New York State, alone among the 50 states, a year-end exam known as the Regents is still offered in a number of courses. A complete review was done of the Regents in the three years prior to Norwich's move to Flexible Modular Scheduling as well as the Regents done in June. Because so few students take the January Regents this was eliminated from the study. The results in all areas of academic testing were extremely positive. Instead of no change being represented in the marks, a dramatic improvement in many areas in Regents testing took place in the first year of flexible scheduling. Before any final conclusions can be drawn, several factors must be taken into consideration. The first is that from year to year the class group varies in ability, intellectual maturity and achievement level irrespective of what the school has or has not achieved with them. Second, program changes, e.g., team teaching in 11th grade English, 9th, 10th, 11th grade math, and other program variables such as new staff, enter into any evaluation results. Finally, from year to year Regents change in their degree of difficulty. For example, even though we feel we have improved our French program considerably by the quality of staff employed and the extensive change in teaching techniques in that program, the French III Regents is acknowledged by all to be very difficult, tending to pull down the marks in that subject area. At the same time some other areas are recognizably easier than in other years.

In balance, however, the Regents testing that took place indicated that Flexible Modular Scheduling was no barrier to students' achieving overall very well on the state Regents exams.

Particularly significant in reviewing the results are:

1. The low rate of failures in English and Social Studies 11.

2. The percentage of "high" passing grades of 80 or better, 69%, in Social Studies 11 Regents.

3. The low failure ratio in the Math 9 Regents relative to other years. Also the high percentage of students, 30%, who achieved a mark of 80% or better in that exam.

4. In Math 10 the lowest percentage rate of failure in four years was achieved with over 67% of the students achieving 80% or better on that exam.

5. Math 11 also showed a low failure ratio and a high 42% number of students achieving 80% or better.

6. French III Regents showed a favorable result compared to 1969 and 1970 results. However, our 1968 Regents results were better.

7. Latin II showed phenomenal results with 51% of the students achieving 80% or better on their Regents. We also achieved the lowest failure rate, 8%, in the past four years.

8. The Spanish program (Spanish III) reflected the best results achieved in four years with 100% of the students achieving 80% or better.

9. The results in Biology are consistent with high scores achieved in other areas; 49% of the students achieved 80% or better on the exam. Our failure ratio was the lowest in the past four years.

10. Perhaps the most striking advancement was seen in the Chemistry area, where 78% of the students achieved 80% or better, with 43% achieving grades in the 90's. Only 5% of the students failed this exam.

11. Physics compared favorably with other years although the percentages were not as striking. A partial explanation is that our senior class did not have a great deal of academic depth, and this is one of the few Regents offered in the senior year.

12. The Typing Regents was down a bit from previous years and we had the greatest number of failures in that area in the past four years.

13. In Business Math, 45% of the students achieved 80% or better, the highest in the four-year span. Results in this area were generally favorable although there was a fairly high failure ratio.

14. Business Law results were consistent with previous years.

15. In Shorthand II and Transcription, 52% of the students achieved 80% or better, well above previous years' totals. Only 20% of the students failed which again was a low percentage relative to prior years.

[The complete results are in the Appendix.]

The message seems clear. The new program, without attempting to factor out individual variables, had been successful in maintaining and indeed improving the student's success in Regents testing. Although this data is rarely used because of the aforementioned complex variables involved, it is useful to know that the opportunities under FMS did not impair an individual student's opportunity to achieve in traditional testing.

PUPIL QUESTIONNAIRES

A number of pupil questionnaires were developed and administered at Norwich to test student reactions to the new schedule. The purpose of testing student reactions is simple—a school schedule which students find to their advantage or like better than another is a valid objective for the staff to reach, as long as it continues to meet other basic instructional requirements. In fact, it is a specific objective of Flexible Modular Scheduling to humanize the school program, breaking down the inherent rigidity of the traditional schedule and dealing with the phenomenon of monotony so rampant in the public schools.

In the area of acceptance it appears that the students show strong support for the new schedule. Three separate surveys were completed. One taken after approximately two weeks of school shows that 83 percent of all the students preferred FMS to the traditional schedule. Negative comments made included the fact that some students no longer had the same lunch hour as their friends, could no longer go home for lunch, or had only one mod for lunch time on certain days.

On another question, dealing with whether or not the transition from the traditional schedule to the six-day modular schedule caused confusion, students indicated only a minor problem. It seems that the extensive preparation was successful.

At mid-year (February 8) a new and much more extensive survey was administered. This survey contained 25 questions, with a possible range of responses including always often sometimes seldom and never. The questions included a number dealing with the instructional aspects of FMS such as large and small group instruction, unassigned time and other areas. Unfortunately, the types of responses requested were not very compatible with the questions asked. That is, a number of questions could have been answered better on a yes-no or more-same-less basis for clearer interpretation.

The results of the questionnaire, grouping a number of questions for convenience are:

> Approximately a third of the students (36%) indicated that they get to see their teachers more often under FMS than previously. Another third (38%)

indicated that they get to see their teachers at least sometimes. 85% indicated that it is "easier" to see the teachers during the school day than previously.

54% indicated that it is easier to see the Guidance Counselors during the school day than previously.

42% of the students indicated that they "often" or "always" used the school resource centers with another third (37%) indicating they use them "sometimes." Only 6% said they never go to resource centers.

The statistics for library usage indicate that 75% of the students use the library "always" or "often." Only 5% indicate they never go. 76% indicate that their use of the library has increased substantially under modular scheduling.

Only 32% of the students say they "often" or "always" go to Commons during their free time. Students feel that about one third (37%) "often" or "always" abuse the privilege. The distribution of students who feel that their use of Commons is reasonable is fairly good. Only 6% feel that student use is "never" reasonable.

A strong majority of the students (79%) feel that they do not have much unassigned time. Only 7%, a very small minority, indicate that they "seldom" or "never" have too much unassigned time. Consistent with that is the very high percentage (88%) who would not want any more structure.

Large group instruction is generally felt (73%) to be an "effective" form of instruction. Conversely a rather high percentage (26%) identify it as "seldom effective" or "never effective." Two-thirds of our students (68%) find small group instruction "always" or "often" an "effective form of instruction." A significantly small percentage (9%) find this a non-effective form of instruction.

Students indicate that only about 4% abuse the two-mod lunch privilege during the open lunch session.

A high percentage (59%) indicate they enjoy school more with FMS than under the traditional schedule. Another two-thirds (60%) indicate that the school day goes faster than in the traditional schedule. In both questions the negative response percentages (15 and 14% respectively) are very low. About 70% of the students felt they were taking advantage of the opportunities offered under FMS. A substantial percentage, however, (29%) felt that they "seldom" or "never" take advantage of the program. Some three-quarters (No. 21) of the students (78%) were "satisfied" with the schedule. Another one-quarter (22%) said that they were not.

Two-thirds (67%) indicate that they are "sometimes," "often," or "always" working harder under FMS. 23% said they "seldom" or "never" work harder.

Support for the six-day cycle was strong, with 87% of the students responding favorably—"often," "always," or "sometimes"—to the six-day cycle, and only 13% voting against it.

Only 8% of the students found the schedule "always" or "often" confusing.

88% of the students indicated a positive reaction to the FMS schedule, with 12% indicating they would like to go back to a traditional schedule.

A final survey, done independently by the school's Student Council, tended to collaborate the earlier studies.

A similar study was made at North East High School, a 2,000-pupil suburban high school in St. Petersburg, Florida, which has been on a modular schedule for a number of years. An evaluation report prepared for the Florida Educational Research Association Conference, January, 1972, is included in the Appendix.

PARENTAL SURVEY

The evaluation of parental attitudes indicates that the reaction to Flexible Modular Scheduling is ambivalent. The reason for this tends to be mixed in nature. Although the disenchantment with schools by the public is high and the need for change is loudly pronounced by the electorate, the types of changes taking place in the schools are towards the liberalization of programs—witness the Informal Education and Schools Without Walls Movement in the elementary schools. Addressing itself to the question of parental attitudes towards the open classroom, *Newsweek* magazine had this to say:

> For taxpayers, boards of education and, most important, parents must all be convinced of the value of the open classroom. And the attitudes of parents are likely, in many cases, to be governed by memories of their own strict schooldays. (What was good enough for me is good enough for my kids.) Many parents equate a quiet school with a good school—and they may even want the schools to instill discipline in their children that they have been unable to develop at home.[14]

At Norwich a serious attempt was made by the school administration to communicate the philosophy and mechanics of the FMS program to parents. All the service clubs were visited, public meetings were held, radio broadcasts and extensive newspaper coverage took place. Many parents accepted and welcomed the new program. Nevertheless, there is always a minority of parents and interested citizens who still do not understand the intent of the program or who are in basic disagreement with its objectives. The amount of opposition to the program was, however, minor. A public meeting was held at the height of a newspaper-generated public controversy over the adoption of the program. A long series of articles in the

---

[14]*Newsweek,* "Does School and Joy = Learning?" May 3, 1971, p. 65. Reprinted by permission.

area newspapers on all aspects of FMS brought the schedule into the public eye. But the meeting was attended by only 22 people not associated with the school, and afterwards an informal discussion indicated that no one present was opposed to the system.

Further, a survey was sent to all senior parents (233) asking them, "If your son (daughter) were able to 'go through' his (her) senior year again, which would you prefer: Flexible Modular Scheduling/Traditional Scheduling? (Check one.)" Of 233 possible returns, *there were only 31* (12%) who favored a return to the "Traditional Schedule." This would indicate a lack of anxiety or concern about FMS on the part of the parents of seniors. It is true that this does not represent an in-depth survey of parental attitudes. Nevertheless, the absence of any organized community opposition, the many favorable comments and the fact that, when given the opportunity to voice their dissent, the public stayed away, would indicate a general acceptance of the program by an otherwise concerned and traditional citizenry.

FACULTY SURVEY

Another specific reason for moving to a Flexible Modular Schedule is that faculties would rather work in a mod pattern than in traditional scheduling. A questionnaire survey asked 38 questions of the faculty in areas covering individualized instruction, large group and small group instruction, student behavior and attitudes, teacher preferences, etc. The answer was a resounding affirmative when the members of the professional staff were polled at Norwich Senior High School.

All the studies completed and reviewed to date point out a consistent trend to favorable reports from the schools using a Flexible Modular Schedule. These positive results offer strong support for the school administrator and faculty who are interested in pursuing the possibility of moving to a Flexible Modular Schedule. It is also interesting to note that a growing body of research is developing as a result of the impetus given the educational establishment by the new scheduling. In this day of accountability by educators to the public and lay boards, far more emphasis must be given to the value of new organizational patterns and techniques. Learning by students is no longer being taken for granted. The answers to questions concerning how a student learns, the value of unstructured time, independent study and individualized instruction play a growing role in determining where we go from here. In attempting to address itself to some of the major problems in conformity and rigidity in schools today, Flexible Modular Scheduling seems to be holding its own and then some.

Summary

The introduction of flexible scheduling will bring cries of "Evaluate!" both from faculty and from parents. Evaluating a program by looking at one variable—the school schedule—is of questionable value; if indeed the program is to be evaluated then the same criteria must be applied evenly to all comparable areas of traditional and flexible schedules. If this is done the question will not be why the school wants to move to a flexible schedule but rather why the school should want to retain the traditional? The school administrator should feel secure that the present data is supportive and may be favorable interpreted. Although it is clear that the research remains sparse, a number of learning studies that have been done show that students in a flexibly scheduled school fare just as well in all respects as their counterparts in the traditional schedule. What is impressive is the data from sources such as opinionnaires, surveys, and observable behavior. Here the trend is clearly and strongly in favor of the new scheduling. Students and faculty both like it much better than a traditional program. Norwich is used as an example to analyze the impact of the new schedule on attendance, dropout rate, academic testing and—most importantly—program improvement.

APPENDIX

**Scheduling
Time Chart**

	Faculty	Scheduling	Data Pro.	Student
Jan.	Development of configuration			Start of course selections
Feb.				
March		Priorities established		End of first phase
		Decisions on # of sections and staffing		
April		Tags made and scheduling tools arranged		
May		Master schedule built		
June	Tentative teacher schedules distributed	Master schedule completed	Master schedule deck punched	All student checked selections
			Course selection deck updated	
July		Students loaded into schedule		
		Master schedule Revised	Master schedule deck updated	
Aug.		All students completely scheduled	Student deck is punched	Summer revision of student course selection
			Final Computer	

Definitions of Terminology

COMMONS: An area set aside in the school where students may relax, eat snacks, study and talk with friends.

DAY CYCLES: Most schedules work on a weekly cycle, using the five days of the week and repeating themselves weekly. A day cycle uses a letter or number for each day and repeats itself on a 4, 6, 9, 10, or 12-day basis. Thus on a six-day letter cycle the schedule begins with "A" day instead of Monday and continues on through "F" day, Monday of the next week. Tuesday now becomes "A" day again, etc.

FREE TIME: Students in a flexibly scheduled school often refer to the unstructured or independent study time as "free time."

INDEPENDENT STUDY: This may have two meanings in a flexibly scheduled school. One refers to the traditional concept of IS, an organized sequential course of study taken by a student, usually out of interest or for credit, with no particular conventional class responsibilities. The second meaning, more germane to a flexibly scheduled school, refers to the unstructured time in a student's schedule during which he has a number of options to choose from.

INDIVIDUALIZED INSTRUCTION: The formalized methodology used by a school to meet individual student needs. This refers to such programs as Learning Activity Packages, UNIPACS, etc.

IN-SCHOOL SUSPENSION: Students involved in serious or continued offenses may be suspended from all classes and will be required to attend structured study hall for the days of suspension.

INSTRUCTIONAL MATERIALS CENTER: The part of a school building which is the main resource center for all subject areas. It should house the main periodical, book and media collections. The IMC should be open to students on a free entry and exit basis during mod breaks. Flexible scheduling usually increases IMC use considerably.

LAB: Regularly scheduled work sessions of a class are usually called labs, are three to four mods in length, and occur once or twice in a cycle.

LARGE GROUP INSTRUCTION: Large group instruction refers to regularly scheduled meetings in the cycle of students from two or more classes combined together. Large groups may be arranged to serve subject matter, departmental, or interdisciplinary purposes.

LUNCH: Lunch refers to a student's unstructured mods during the time designated as lunch time. Usually specific mods are designed, e.g., modes 8-12 inclusive, every day. A student can go to lunch any time during this period, but school policy may restrict the number of mods he takes for this purpose. Students will usually have two mods for lunch during this time. Some, because of a heavy schedule, will have a single lunch mod on some days.

MINI-COURSES: Either students or teachers may request that a short, non-credit course be given. These courses are conducted during unstructured time and may be given on almost any topic.

MOD: A unit of time used in place of the normal period. They are shorter and there are more of them in a day. Schools may use a mod of any length although ten minutes seems to be the minimum and 30 the maximum. At NSHS the mod is 22 minutes long and there are 18 of them in a day.

MOD BREAK: The mod break is the passing time to the next class following the end of the last mod of the scheduled meeting.

MODES OF INSTRUCTION: Instruction in a flexibily scheduled school is based on grouping of students into large groups, small groups, laboratories, regular classes. These are known as phases or modes of instruction.

OPEN LABS: Some departments have established labs where students may go during unstructured time to do school work. Open labs are found in art, industrial arts, home economics, foreign language, and business.

OUT-OF-SCHOOL SUSPENSION: Students who continue to be involved in disciplinary action may be suspended for any length of time up to a week. In most cases state law requires formal hearings and expulsion procedures for periods longer than a week.

PHASES: See Modes of Instruction.

QUIET STUDY: An area set aside for traditional quiet study. As is true in other optional areas in a flexibly scheduled school, no attendance is taken and students are free to come and go on the mod break.

REGULAR CLASS: Typically a group of 25 to 30 students is called a regular class meeting.

RESOURCE CENTER: A supplementary learning center which houses materials, resources or equipment for a particular discipline. Staffed by faculty members on their unassigned time, it is open for students to do work related to the subject or to come for assistance.

SMALL GROUPS: Regularly scheduled meetings of half a class group—the teacher and 8 to 14 students.

STRUCTURED STUDY: Students unable to use their unstructured time wisely will have it taken from them. They will be "structured" into a study hall which is supervised and where attendance is taken.

UNSTRUCTURED TIME: Those mods during the day when a student is not required or scheduled to report to any class are considered unstructured. During this time students may go to a great variety of areas. Students must report to these areas on time and once there they must stay until the end of the mod.

WORK AREAS: Each department has established work areas for students where help in that specific area is available. Students may go to these areas freely during their unstructured mods. Students may be assigned to them as part of their class work or as a result of failure to meet minimum course requirements. Work areas may be synonymous with area resource centers, labs, etc.

Westinghouse Learning Corporation
Educational Data Services

SCHEDULING CONTRACT FOR A COMPUTER-BUILT MASTER SCHEDULE

Westinghouse Learning Corporation agrees to provide to_____
the following services for the 1973-74 school year:

I   Basic Service

A.   Utilize a modular school scheduling program which, when provided with
      school parameters, teacher lists, room lists, course structures and
      student course requests, will schedule the described resources of the
      school within the parameters of the scheduling program. The school
      scheduling program will include a logic check of the school's input,
      the generation of a master schedule, the ability to make manual
      changes in the master schedule, the assignment of students to classes
      except for unresolvable conflicts, and the ability to make changes
      in student course requests; and provide the school with a master
      schedule, student, teacher, and room schedules, and class lists.

B.   The above services will be provided at the following cost to the
      school:

      10-32 periods (modules)

Number of Students Processed	Cost	Base Price
699 or less	$1,300.00 plus	$5.00 per student over 240*
700-999	$3,700.00 plus	$3.00 per student over 700*
1,000 plus	$4,600.00 plus	$2.00 per student over 1,000*

      9 or less periods

Number of Students Processed	Cost	Base Price
999 or less	$1,200.00 plus	$2.30 per student over 400*
1,000 plus	$2,600.00 plus	$1.80 per student over 1,000*

C.   The Basic Service to the School Will Include:

1.   Two copies of the manual of directions for the school administrator (additional copies available at $10.00 per copy)
2.   Keypunching of school parameters (deck 1), course enrollment transfers (deck 2), course combinations (deck 3), Teacher Lists (deck 4), room lists (deck 5), and course data packet (deck 6)
3.   Optical scanning of student request (deck 7)
4.   Providing a course enrollment tally
5.   Four master schedule construction runs
6.   The cost for travel and expenses for two trips by an educational consultant to the school site
7.   Two consultant days at the school site. Additional technical consultant time at the school will be made available at a cost of $125.00 per day to the school plus expenses. Additional consultant time at the consultant's office will be made available at no charge.
8.   A final master schedule, teacher and room schedules-4 copies
9.   Student schedules with pupil name, grade, and sex information on schedule-4 copies
10. Class lists-3 copies; Homeroom lists-3 copies
11. A tally of lunch assignments
12. A tally of the number of students assigned to courses each module of the day, each day of the cycle
13. A list of students having schedules with conflicts
14. A technical workshop: Phase I- Input preparation (Mid-December)
                             Phase II- Output interpretation

II. Optional Services

Check Optional
Services Requested

A. Additional pupil information printed on
schedules and pupil directories @$.20/pupil **A.** _____

    1. Information on student schedules
        a. Homeroom   e. General information
        b. Locker number   f. Parent's name
        c. Telephone   g. Address
        d. Educational classification   h. Date of birth
    2. Pupil grade directory -4 copies
    3. Homeroom list -4 copies
    4. School roster -4 copies

B. Provide punched class cards for input to a grade
reporting system. One card per pupil per course-
phase and course-phase header cards are provided.
Charge waived if in WLC Grade Reporting Service. @$.20/pupil **B.** _____

C. Additional pupil, teacher, and room
schedules -4 copies @$.20/pupil **C.** _____

D. Additional class lists -2 copies @$.15/pupil **D.** _____

E. Pupil information and request verification
report @$.15/pupil **E.** _____

F. Course List - students registered for each
course   9 or less periods @$.10/pupil F.(a) _____
              10 or more periods @$.15/pupil F.(b) _____

G. Unscheduled student list (included in @$.01/pupil/
Basic Service for schools with 9 periods   module desired
or less) $.05/pupil minimum   G. _____

H. Course Conflict Matrix (maximum of 200
courses can be included) @$.05/pupil **H.** _____

I. Multiple Term Scheduling
    a. Semester or 2-term master schedule (10% of basic service) I.(a). _____
    b. 3-term master schedule   (18% of basic service) I.(b). _____
    c. Quarter or 4-term master schedule (24% of basic service) I.(c). _____

J. Student Term Assignment Registrar - STAR
    a. Semester or 2-term master schedule (6% of basic service) J.(a) _____
    b. 3-term master schedule   (8% of basic service) J.(b) _____
    c. Quarter or 4-term master schedule (10% of basic service) J.(c) _____

K. _____ **K.** _____

L. _____ **L.** _____

The school shall designate someone to coordinate and maintain an orderly flow of information and materials in cooperation with the WLC Consultant. This person should have the necessary authority to make related decisions as needed and should be available to make such decisions.

The terms of payment of this agreement are as follows:
Estimated 50% of the cost is due and payable within 45 days of the delivery of the first SSP. The balance is due 45 days after the invoice date following the final delivery of the requested services. All transportation fees are to be paid by the contracting school.

This working agreement can be established by signing the acceptance below and returning it to WLC.

Number of students anticipated for 1973-74:_____
Final charges will be based on the actual number of students using the scheduling service.

Accepted by:

_____
School Representative

_____
Position

_____
Date

Send invoices to:

_____

_____

_____

_____
WLC Representative

Date_____

Mail to:

Educational Data Services
Westinghouse Learning Corporation
2938 Hempstead Turnpike
Levittown, New York 11756

Phone: 212-983-5345

* These prices are subject to change without notice until such time as dated and signed by a WLC representative.

Developing the Course Configuration:
A Faculty Packet

PACKET OBJECTIVES

1. To identify the modes of instruction for each course in a given department.
2. To develop a configuration for courses at each grade level of teaching.

IDENTIFYING TERMS

Modes of instruction refers to the different student-meeting patterns or group organizations used by a school in a learning program. They usually meet in the following patterns:

- —Large group (more than 40 students)
- —Small group (10 to 15)
- —Regular class (20 to 40)
- —Labs (20 to 40 in a work situation)
- —Individualized instruction (1 or 5)
- —Independent study. (Ex.—extension course, programmed instruction, home study).

Configuration refers to the time, sequence and combination of patterns to be given the various modes of instruction. It is always drawn in the manner in which the student would go through the cycle.

Example:

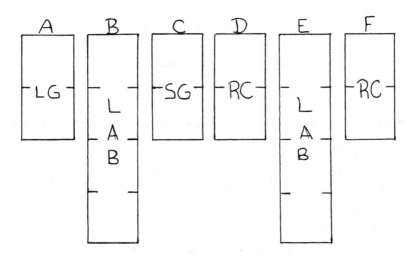

Figure A-1
Biology Configuration

Developing the Modes of Instruction

Directions:

1. Departments should meet to determine the learning objectives for each course to be taught by the members in the department.

2. Determine the total amount of time necessary to meet the course learning objectives (for each course) using all modes of instruction.

3. Determine the modes of instruction to be used in the course.

4. Plot these on your worksheet.

5. Indicate specific restrictions to be considered—room use, lab set-up time, team teaching staff meetings, day independence, etc.

Suggestions:

In attempting to determine modes of instruction and course configurations, the following should serve as guidelines:

1. Check to see how much time you are presently using (clock minutes).

2. What are your present modes employed?

3. What advantage will there be to employing new modes for this department offering?

4. How much structured class time could be relinquished from the present time allotment?

5. Do you have sufficient material designed for the course to allow students to work *independently* in the library or resource centers during increased IS time?

6. Remember that when using large groups you decrease the teacher's formal classroom time; when going to small groups you increase the time.

7. You should not try to "schedule" IS meeting time for individual students but you should calculate the time.

8. Be sure you are familiar with the general administrative scheduling restrictions.

General administrative scheduling restrictions

1. All sections of the same subject must use the same configuration.

2. No course should exceed in time its present time allotment (traditional schedule) to a six-day cycle.

3. By increasing the cycle to six days, a department desiring to meet the students every day must be prepared to decrease its total time to meet #2.

4. No meeting should be more than five mods in length on any given day.

5. Do not "insist" on a request such as LG mods 1 and 2 "only" on a day because scheduling difficulties may be a factor. Rather request LG, AM, DAY A, etc. Put your preference for the specific mods in parenthesis after the morning or afternoon designation.

6. Passing time of four minutes is included in the last meeting mods. Thus, a two-mod class runs 40 minutes (22 + 22 = 44 - 4 = 40).

7. For the purposes of planning, your subject teacher is to assume that he will be teaching the same course(s) next year unless notified specifically otherwise.

KEY: LAB — Labs
      LG —   Large group
      SG —   Small group
      DAYS —   A, B, C, D, E, F

Some faculty considerations

1. Some schools base the length of the module on the optimum length of a lecture period, which seems to run around 25 to 28 minutes. Studies concluded at Stanford University indicate that pupil attention falls off sharply after about 28 minutes of teacher presentation.

2. Radical departures in time allocation in a given area should be commensurate with the philosophy, skill, training and materials development of that course, teacher or department. Said another way, there is no point in reducing class time 75% if you don't have backup materials such as LAPS, Unipacs or other resources to fill the vacuum.

SCHEDULING PRIORITIES: It usually is not possible for us to achieve all that is asked in departmental scheduling specifications. List below in priority order the scheduling request most important in your department.

1. _____
2. _____
3. _____
4. _____
5. _____

SCHEDULING COMPROMISES: We have listed below the kinds of scheduling compromises we expect to have to make to resolve conflicts. Use a simple code to indicate how you view these. Please remember that we are referring to only a *few* students and then only as a last resort.

Fine: Does not constitute a serious problem with us.
O.K.: Accept with reluctance
NO: Positively not acceptable under any circumstances.

_____1. Student may substitute IS for part of class module.
_____2. Student may omit small group.
_____3. Student may omit large group.
_____4. Student may be in small group with same teacher, same ability group, different students.
_____5. Student may be in large group different from class.
_____6. Student may be in lab with same teacher, different class, same ability group.
_____7. Student may be scheduled in phases of two different classes with same teacher, same ability group.

Day Independence: In order to facilitate scheduling, to what extent may two of the three or more phases of a course (sg, class, lab, lg) meet in the same day?

_____
_____

Are there any special requests for restrictions *affecting* the course structures or scheduling that you would like us to consider?

_____
_____

REGULAR CLASS* TO MOD CONVERSION TABLE FOR FMS–SIX-DAY CYCLE

The number of 22-minute mods
needed in a six-day cycle to
achieve parity.

Meeting in Traditional Class*	100%	90%	80%	70%	65%
10 times per week	27	23	21	19	17
7 times per week	19	17	15	13	12
6 times per week	18	14	13	11	10
5 times per week	14	13	11	10	9
4 times per week	11	10	9	8	7
3 times per week	9	8	7	6	6
2 times per week	6	5	5	4	4

*Based on use of 47-minute period.

EXAMPLE OF CONVERSION

Regular Schedule: Class Meets

Once a day
Five times per week
47 minutes each meeting
Total time five days–235 min.

When converted to a six-day cycle

Add 47 minutes for a total of
282 minutes.

Then calculate correct equivalent number of 22-minute mods:

```
  22
  14    (no. of mods found through trial and error)
 308    (total length of time inclusive of passing time)
- 24    (4 minutes passing x 6 days)
 284    TOTAL MINUTES MODULAR SCHEDULE
```

THIS IS ROUNDED OFF TO 100% EQUIVALENT TIME.

FACULTY
WORK SHEET

Tentative Configuration
To be submitted for Each Course

Department_____ Course _____
Teacher(s)_____

1					
2					
3					
4					
5					

HORIZONTAL: A, B, C, D, E, F,—Six-Day Cycle
VERTICAL: 1 2 3 4 5

Add Special Considerations

No. of Team Planning Mods _____
Set-up Time   _____
Others   _____

AN EVALUATION REPORT ON THE
MODULAR SCHEDULE OF NORTHEAST
HIGH SCHOOL, ST. PETERSBURG, FLORIDA

Henry F. Raichle
Research and Development Department
Pinellas County Schools
Clearwater, Florida

A paper presented at the Florida Educational Research Association Conference, January 29, 1972, in Ft. Lauderdale, Florida.

TABLE OF CONTENTS

INTRODUCTION

Northeast High School is a three-year coeducational senior high school situated in a surburban section of St. Petersburg. The students, 2,035, for the most part are from the middle and upper middle socioeconomic strata. Academically, tests indicate that their abilities range from the lower quarter to the 99th percentile.

The faculty is composed of 99 classroom teachers, 56 men and 43 women, 4 guidance counselors, a dean of boys, a dean of girls, a registrar, a curriculum associate, an assistant principal and principal.

Northeast High has been operating on a complete school-wide modular schedule for the past two and one-half school years. The schedule was developed by the faculty, the Research and Development staff and the University of Florida's Computing Center. The day is composed of 20 twenty-minute modules beginning at 8:00 a.m. and ending at 2:40 p.m., with a 15-minute home room period prior to beginning classes.

The students and faculty are unscheduled about one-third of the time. During the unscheduled time, students may choose to go to the media center, to any one of six resource centers, meet individually with teachers, discussion commons, or may leave the campus (open-campus).

The school has 6 large group rooms, 50 regular size classrooms, and 20 small group rooms. The small group rooms were constructed by dividing a regular size classroom with a partition. The auditorium is scheduled for some large groups. The facility also includes a 10,000 square foot media center and 6 other resource centers for Language Arts, Social Studies, Science-Math Technology, Business Education, Foreign Language, and Driver Training.

Team teaching is used in Language Arts, Social Studies, Math, Science, Foreign Language and most nonacademic subjects. Large group sizes range from 50 to 180 students. Generally, the large groups are teacher-oriented and are usually no longer than 40 minutes.

A second mode of instruction is the regular size grouping which is teacher-student oriented and ranges from 20 to 40 in size. This mode of instruction usually consists of laboratory experiences and traditional classroom activities.

The third mode of learning takes place in small groups, with an average group size of 16. These groups are student-oriented in which students are engaged in seminar-type activities. These 3 sizes of groupings operate within the 20 modules, each subject having a variety of number of mods.

Much of the merit of this program lies in the unscheduled time during which students may study independently, schedule teachers or guidance counselors for a one-to-one personal conference, and work on individual interests in open-laboratories or resource centers. This unscheduled time allows each student the flexibility to self-schedule approximately one-third of his time.

Each major discipline has a resource center. These centers are staffed by teachers and paraprofessionals. Students can study in the resource centers individually or in groups. In these centers students can work on assignments and receive help directly from a staff member of that department. One favorable result of the resource centers is that a student may receive assistance from a teacher in that discipline regardless of whether or not that student has a class with the teacher. Almost all departments are team planned and they know what kinds of experiences are going on within their team.

Another place a student can go during his unstructured time is the media center. It is basically a place to do research, read magazines and books, listen to music, view enrichment films or, through the carrel system, become absorbed in his own quiet spot. Students may also hear a recorded lecture they have missed or wish to review.

There is also a discussion commons. This is another option for the student to choose during his unstructured time. He can sit down and talk with friends.

A desirable feature of the unscheduled time is the open-lab. Students may use this activity to continue laboratory experiments or work on individual projects. However, due to the heavy schedule of classes in these areas, these opportunities are limited.

A student may go to the guidance office. Traditionally scheduled schools have difficulty in arranging appointments with individual students as they must schedule them during regular class, interrupting the students and teachers. Guidance people have more time to counsel with students.

The philosophy that forms the basis for Northeast High School's educational program is that education can be an experience in which students take control of some of their own learning experiences and learn how to handle them. Education doesn't have to be something they dread, but it isn't all fun and games either.

This departure from a traditional high school program has allowed students at Northeast High School more opportunities to make decisions about their own educational experiences and allows teachers more flexibility in planning and using different approaches to instruction.

The following report reflects the results of this program to date.

ACADEMIC ACHIEVEMENT

During February and March, 1971, the Stanford Achievement Test: High School Battery, was administered to a sample of 11th grade students drawn from Northeast High School and two other Pinellas County High Schools (Boca Ciega and Clearwater) as part of a senior high school assessment project. From this project it was determined that Northeast High School students did not achieve significantly greater or less than students at the other two Pinellas County High Schools. These students were representative of students that have been in Pinellas County schools for the entire period of their secondary schooling.

The purpose of this testing was to determine how students who have taken their secondary schooling in Pinellas County schools rank with respect to national norms and to each other in the areas of English, numerical competence, algebra I—geometry, reading, science, social studies, and spelling.

Results of the tests indicated that in the areas of English, numerical competence, social studies, and spelling, Pinellas County students were at the level of national norms. No significant differences at the 95 percent level of confidence were found among the three Pinellas County high schools.

In the areas of algebra I—geometry and science, Pinellas students tested significantly above national norm levels. This result was consistently high in all three high schools with no significant differences (among schools) at the 95 percent level of confidence.

In the area of reading the Pinellas County sample tested significantly below the national norm. No significant differences were found among the schools at the 95 percent level of confidence. The Research and Development Department will continue a longitudinal study of academic achievement at Northeast High as well as monitoring the program's effectiveness on other desirable outcomes.

STUDENT ATTITUDES

A survey of student attitudes toward modular scheduling was given in May, 1971. This was the third survey of student attitudes taken during the two years of modular scheduling at Northeast High. The two previous surveys were given in October, 1969 and May, 1970.

The general attitude of students, as indicated by these series of questionnaires, has shown increasing acceptance to almost total (95%) preference of the modular over the traditional schedule. The student responses indicate a steady growth in the application of the basic principles upon which modular scheduling is based—to facilitate individualized learning. For example, responses to questions 3, 4, 5, 9 and 13 indicate that students feel very positive about the environmental conditions for learning under the modular schedule. Over 80% of the students felt that they had more individual contact with teachers as a result of modular scheduling. A significant majority (84%) also feel that open campus has helped develop responsibility. Almost all students (96%) felt that they had more opportunity to complete their homework and study during school hours.

Two student comments of note included:

"I have less tension than I've ever had going to school. I find school very interesting and for the first time in a long time I really enjoy going to school."

"Open campus has really done things for the students. It helps to get things off your mind, when you can just take a walk and think things over."

The following tabulation is a summary of the response of each question on the Student Survey of May, 1971. Detailed breakdowns of responses by grade level are available from the Research and Development Department.

NORTHEAST MODULAR SCHEDULE STUDENT SURVEY
SUMMARY OF ALL RESPONSES

Below please mark the choice best describing your opinion:
1.) = modular schedule; 2.) = no difference; 3.) = traditional schedule

1623 Responses
Response Shown
as % of Total

		1	2	3
3. I make better use of my study time in the	3.	86	10	4
4. I have a better opportunity to learn at my own rate of speed under the	4.	87	10	3
5. I develop more responsibility and self-discipline in the	5.	85	11	3
6. I find school more interesting with the	6.	93	5	2
7. I have less tension and anxiety in the	7.	74	19	7
8. My attitude to "school in general" is better with the	8.	83	14	3
9. I have more opportunity to use the library facilities in the	9.	84	14	1
10. I check out more library reference materials in the	10.	36	57	7
11. My choice of course offerings is greater with the	11.	72	26	2
12. I have more opportunity to complete my homework and study during school hours in the	12.	96	3	1
13. I have more individual contact with my teachers in the	13.	82	13	4

(THESE STATEMENTS REQUIRE THAT YOU SELECT FROM THESE THREE CHOICES)

1.) = yes; 2.) = no difference; 3.) = no

		1	2	3
14. Open campus has helped me develop more responsibility	14.	84	14	2
15. I have adequate opportunity to discuss my goals and academic problems with the guidance department	15.	66	25	9
16. My attention to a lecture or discussion is greater in a 40 minute class than in a 55 minute one	16.	87	12	1
17. I learn more effectively with variations of class size and time	17.	82	14	4
18. The present lunch schedule is better than the one I've had in previous years	18.	78	16	6
19. I have sufficient unscheduled time	19.	83	3	14
20. I prefer to choose between a la carte and class "A" lunches	20.	76	19	5

		1	2	3
21.	I have adequate opportunity to participate in small group discussion	21.	88	10	2
22.	I prefer the modular schedule over the traditional one	22.	95	2	2

If you care to offer additional comments
please use a separate sheet of paper

THANK YOU FOR YOUR TIME

TEACHER ATTITUDES

As teachers have worked with this totally new program over the two year period there have been marked changes in their personal feelings for the program and its effects on students. A series of three surveys given over the two years indicate teachers at Northeast High generally feel that their environment for teaching has improved significantly under modular scheduling.

Most teachers surveyed (85%) favored teaching under modular scheduling with a majority (66%) stating that they significantly favored teaching under the modular schedule. Teachers also indicated that some of the basic principles upon which modular scheduling is based are operating successfully. The increased opportunities for teachers to work individually with students (question 5) is a strong indicator of the opportunities inherent in the modular schedule to facilitate learning.

Teachers are not as strong in their opinion as students are relating to how well students are assuming more responsibility for their own behavior and education (questions 2 and 8). Two-thirds of the teachers, however, feel that modular scheduling does influence these areas more favorably than traditional scheduling.

The following is a summary of the April 1971 teacher survey.

NORTHEAST MODULAR SCHEDULE TEACHER SURVEY
SUMMARY OF RESPONSES

Using the scale provided, rate each item from 1 to 5:
1) Significantly more on modular scheduling; 2) Somewhat more on modular scheduling; 3) No difference; 4) Somewhat more on traditional scheduling; 5) Significantly more on traditional scheduling.

96 Responses
Response Shown as % of Total

		1	2	3	4	5	No Response
1.	I feel that I am able to help students learn my subject.	1.	41	36	10	8	4	1

2. Student behavior in class is better.	2.	39	23	31	2	1	4
3. There is opportunity to exchange ideas with colleagues.	3.	40	33	21	4	1	1
4. Student general attitude is favorable toward school and teachers.	4.	33	48	13	4	2	0
5. There is opportunity to work individually with students.	5.	66	23	5	2	1	3
6. There is opportunity to use more effective methods and techniques.	6.	45	29	20	3	2	1
7. There is opportunity to use media more effectively.	7.	27	42	23	6	0	20
8. Students assume responsibility.	8.	18	42	28	9	3	0
9. Teachers are really able to communicate with students.	9.	27	39	24	2	2	6
10. All things considered, I favor teaching.	10.	66	19	4	4	2	5

PROGRAM COSTS

The tabulation below compares the operating expenditures of three Pinellas County senior high schools during the 1969-70 school year. The 1969-70 expenditures do not include computer time provided by the University of Florida's Computing Center whose services were provided gratis during the research and development phase. Expenditures do include approximately 1,000 manhours of the Research and Development staff time in developing the master schedule, redesign of the physical facilities and staff development. It is estimated that the 1970-71 expenditure per pupil at Northeast High will be slightly higher than for Clearwater and Boca Ciega High Schools due to additional computer services costs of approximately $2.00 per pupil.

Operational Costs at
Three Pinellas County High Schools
1969-70

High Schools	Total Expenditures	Number of Pupils	Cost per Pupil
Clearwater	$1,273,134	2,118	$601
Boca Ciega	1,152,797	1,998	577
Northeast	1,173,657	1,966	597

OTHER FACTORS

In March, 1971, the Northeast High School staff prepared a report on factors related to student outcomes of their educational program. The following tabulations are extracted from this report.

Grade Distribution

Spanning four school administrations, the grade distribution has remained fairly stable, with a definite trend upward apparent this year.
All Subjects—First Semester (Percentages)

Year	A	B	C	D	F
64-65	8.1	25.1	36.5	18.0	8.3
65-66	9.4	25.4	36.0	21.5	6.4
66-67	8.9	26.1	35.3	20.4	7.9
67-68	(not available first semester)				
68-69	(not available first semester)				
69-70	10.0	24.0	31.0	20.0	11.0
70-71	11.0	29.0	32.0	19.0	6.0

Florida Twelfth Grade Placement Tests

The class of 1971 represents the first senior group to reflect modular scheduling since they were tested in September of this year. An obvious decrease in the number scoring below 100 and an increase in those scoring above 250 is encouraging. Ninety-one percent of the senior class takes this test.

Class	% above 250	% above 300	% below 100
1967	62.0	51.0	8.0
1968	60.0	48.0	8.0
1969	61.0	46.0	8.0
1970	56.1	44.2	14.0
1971	57.0	44.0	10.0
1972	63.0	50.0	7.0

Drop-out Comparison

The principal and staff feel that the Modular Schedule does not, as yet, appear to have an increased holding power for students. If anything it tends to identify the drop-out a little more quickly. Curriculum changes, with the addition of courses designed to meet the needs of the non-college bound, have been added and more of those courses are still a high priority need.

Daily Attendance Comparison

ADA for the two and one-half years on modular scheduling has been consistent with that reported for previous years with no more than a 1% variance from month to month.

Skipping of Classes

A detailed study by the deans this year confirmed the fact that there is no more extensive classroom skipping than under a traditional schedule. Actually, the problem is now limited to a smaller percentage of the student body. The fact that other types of behavior problems, such as class disruption, smoking in restrooms, etc., are almost nonexistent seemed to make the skipping appear more of a problem than the facts substantiate.

Open Campus

The staff feels that an open campus is a necessary element for the success of a modular schedule. Many of the problems of last year are not present with an open campus. Smoking in the building, vandalism, and hallway congestion are not evident this year. There has been no marked increase in class tardies as might be expected. Our community has apparently accepted the open campus.

All indications point to the fact that an overwhelming majority of the students are accepting the responsibilities placed on them. The attitude of students toward teachers and school in general is positive. They appear to be proud of their school program and are quick to respond to requests for improvement in areas of concern to the administration.

Lunch Program

The modular scheduling has allowed a unique lunch (and breakfast) schedule. Unlike other food service programs in the county's senior high schools the varying blocks of unscheduled time allow students to participate in breakfast served from 7:15 to 9:00 a.m. Each student has a scheduled lunch period between 11:00 a.m. and 1:00 p.m. which allows them to participate in either the a-la-carte or class "A" lunch program. The staff feels that this program better meets the needs of students for food services.

Use of Unscheduled Time

A survey of the number of student-teacher conferences held during unscheduled time indicates that for the most part this time is being used effectively. Some teachers have more requests for individual help than others by virtue of the subject matter with which they deal. Obviously, some students require more individual instruction. At present they appear to be realizing more benefits at the remedial level than at the advanced stage where more of the outstanding students should be encouraged into independent projects beyond the scope of the normal high school program.

Use of Media Center and Resource Areas

The atmosphere of the Media Center has changed from the idea of a quiet hide-away to a center of activity. Students seem to feel that it really is their center, taking advantage more and more of the enrichment activities that are provided via motion pictures, filmstrips, and records. On an average, 1,168 students use the center daily. The average daily book check-out for home is less than previously which is probably related to the fact that many books are now available through the individual resource centers which operate at near capacity throughout the day, and to better use of student time.

Parent Advisory Committee

The Parent Advisory Committee, which numbers approximately 25, has been most enthusiastic in its endorsement of the modular schedule, expressing the viewpoint that it is a partial answer to student unrest.

SUMMARY AND RECOMMENDATIONS

Summary

Generally, students have favored to a greater degree than teachers the modular scheduling in all three surveys taken over the past two years. Students' attitudes have progressed from a majority favoring modular scheduling to almost total acceptance in the most recent survey.

Teachers, at first reluctant to fully accept modular scheduling, have over the two years increasingly endorsed the conditions of teaching and learning which have been provided by the modular schedule.

Student outcomes in terms of academic achievement indicate no significant gains or losses during the two-year period compared with other Pinellas County high schools.

The significant gains during this initial development period have been in the affective domain, i.e., gains in students' attitudes toward learning and their school environment and development of individual responsibility for making choices from among alternatives.

While the Research and Development staff and the University of Florida's Computing Center staff were instrumental in initially developing the system for successfully operating a modular schedule, the Northeast High School staff has taken over the function of constructing the master schedule and sectioning students with the mechanical assistance of the computer for the 1971-72 school year.

Recommendations

1. Further staff development on individualized learning processes be included in 1971-72 for the Northeast High School staff.

2. Provisions should be made for a planned calendar of orientation of all aspects of modular scheduling for visitation teams of staff members from all Pinellas County secondary schools. These visits would serve as an initial staff development phase of countywide implementation of modular scheduling.

3. Continued review of course time requirements, approaches to instruction and content needs to be made.

4. Improve procedures for structuring the unscheduled time of those few students who are unable to use this time effectively.

5. Increased pupil contact time with guidance counselors is needed. Unscheduled pupil and counselor time allows a rare opportunity to try innovative counseling.

6. Continued review by the school's staff of total course offerings to ensure that the total program is meeting needs of all students.

7. Continued longitudinal study to ascertain the maintaining of student achievement and personal rewards of this type of educational program.

Four-Year-Comparative Study
at Norwich Senior High School

        The following tables represent a four-year comparative study of the Iowa test scores and New York State Regents achievement marks for pupils at Norwich Senior High School 1968-1971. June, 1971, completed the school's first full year in a modular schedule.

IOWA TESTS OF EDUCATIONAL DEVELOPMENT
COMPARISON—FOUR CLASSES OF SOPHOMORES

GRADE EQUIVALENT SCORES

Class	COMPOSITE	Comprehension	Vocabulary	READING TOTAL	Usage	Spelling	LANGUAGE ARTS TOTAL	MATHEMATICS	SOCIAL STUDIES	SCIENCE	USE OF SOURCES
'70	11.6	11.1	11.4			10.8	11.1	11.9	12.1	12.2	
'71	11.3	11.1	11.2			10.7	10.5	11.8	11.8	11.6	
'72	11.4	10.8	11.3			11.1	10.9	11.7	11.4	11.9	
'73	11.4	11.1	11.4			11.1	10.7	11.8	11.6	11.9	

% iles — NATIONAL NORMS

Class	COMPOSITE	Comprehension	Vocabulary	READING TOTAL	Usage	Spelling	LANGUAGE ARTS TOTAL	MATHEMATICS	SOCIAL STUDIES	SCIENCE	USE OF SOURCES
'70	70	68	64	68	54	54	54	71	70	69	69
'71	64	63	64	63	54	54	54	62	64	63	59
'72	64	63	57	63	54	54	54	71	64	57	64
'73	64	68	64	68	54	54	54	67	64	57	64

IOWA TESTS OF EDUCATIONAL DEVELOPMENT
COMPARISON—FOUR CLASSES OF SENIORS

GRADE EQUIVALENT SCORES

Class	COMPOSITE	Comprehension	Vocabulary	READING TOTAL	Usage	Spelling	LANGUAGE ARTS TOTAL	MATHEMATICS	SOCIAL STUDIES	SCIENCE	USE OF SOURCES
'68	12.3		11.9	12.1			12.2	11.7	12.5	11.9	12.6
'69	11.9		11.8	11.7			11.8	11.2	12.4	11.8	12.5
'70	12.2		11.7	11.9			11.8	11.7	12.4	12.1	12.6
'71	12.1		11.8	12.3			11.8	11.3	11.7	11.9	12.4

% iles — NATIONAL NORMS

Class	COMPOSITE	Comprehension	Vocabulary	READING TOTAL	Usage	Spelling	LANGUAGE ARTS TOTAL	MATHEMATICS	SOCIAL STUDIES	SCIENCE	USE OF SOURCES
'68	70	62	66	62	63	63	63	72	62	59	65
'69	59	52	65	52	57	57	57	64	57	54	60
'70	65	57	60	57	57	57	57	72	57	65	65
'71	59	57	66	62	57	44	51	64	53	59	55

IOWA TESTS OF EDUCATIONAL DEVELOPMENT
COMPARISON—FOUR CLASSES OF JUNIORS

GRADE EQUIVALENT SCORES

Class	COMPOSITE	Comprehension	Vocabulary	READING TOTAL	Usage	Spelling	LANGUAGE ARTS TOTAL	MATHEMATICS	SOCIAL STUDIES	SCIENCE	USE OF SOURCES
'69	11.8		11.5	11.4			11.6	11.2	12.3	11.7	12.3
'70	11.9		11.6	11.7			11.6	11.2	12.3	11.9	12.5
'71	11.8		11.5	11.6			11.3	11.2	12.2	11.9	12.5
'72	11.8		11.5	11.8			11.5	11.1	12.2	11.9	12.4

% iles NATIONAL NORMS

Class	COMPOSITE	Comprehension	Vocabulary	READING TOTAL	Usage	Spelling	LANGUAGE ARTS TOTAL	MATHEMATICS	SOCIAL STUDIES	SCIENCE	USE OF SOURCES
'69	66	59	61	59	59	59	59	69	65	58	64
'70	66	59	68	59	59	59	59	69	70	64	69
'71	66	59	61	59	52	52	52	69	65	64	64
'72	66	64	61	64	59	59	59	65	65	58	64

English 11

Range	1968 Totals	%	1969 Totals	%	1970 Totals	%	1971 Totals	%
100-90	14	9%	12	10%	13	9%	8	7%
89-80	28	18%	24	21%	25	18%	23	21%
79-70	31	20%	38	33%	37	26%	40	37%
69-65	37	23%	20	17%	35	25%	23	21%
Fail	48	30%	22	19%	30	21%	14	12%
	158	100%	116	100%	140	99%	108	98%

Social Studies 11

Range	1968 Totals	%	1969 Totals	%	1970 Totals	%	1971 Totals	%
100-90	4	3%	8	7%	47	35%	44	33%
89-80	23	16%	28	23%	48	36%	47	36%
79-70	65	46%	47	38%	30	22%	31	23%
69-65	17	12%	16	13%	9	7%	5	4%
Fail	32	23%	23	19%	1	1%	3	2%
	141	100%	122	100%	135	100%	130	98%

Math 9

Range	1968 Totals	%	1969 Totals	%	1970 Totals	%	1971 Totals	%
100-90	1	3%	-	-	-	-	7	17%
89-80	2	5%	4	6%	3	9%	5	13%
79-70	5	13%	4	6%	7	22%	8	20%
69-65	5	13%	7	11%	7	22%	8	20%
Fail	26	67%	49	77%	15	47%	12	30%
	39	101%	64	100%	32	100%	40	100%

Math 10

Range	1968 Totals	%	1969 Totals	%	1970 Totals	%	1971 Totals	%
100-90	22	20%	11	9%	30	25%	44	38%
89-80	26	24%	31	24%	21	17%	34	29%
79-70	21	19%	37	29%	24	20%	18	16%
69-65	21	19%	15	12%	4	3%	8	7%
Fail	18	17%	35	37%	43	35%	12	10%
	108	99%	129	101%	122	100%	116	100%

Math 11

Range	1968 Totals	%	1969 Totals	%	1970 Totals	%	1971 Totals	%
100-90	15	11%	15	17%	17	16%	28	27%
89-80	30	23%	11	13%	27	25%	16	15%
79-70	29	22%	26	30%	30	28%	27	26%
69-65	23	18%	17	20%	16	15%	17	17%
Fail	34	26%	18	21%	16	15%	15	15%
	131	100%	87	101%	106	99%	103	100%

French 111

Range	1968 Totals	%	1969 Totals	%	1970 Totals	%	1971 Totals	%
100-90	12	24%	4	18%	6	14%	4	9%
89-80	20	29%	3	14%	7	16%	13	30%
79-70	12	24%	5	23%	12	27%	11	25%
69-65	4	8%	5	23%	5	11%	6	14%
Fail	3	6%	5	23%	14	32%	9	20%
	51	101%	22	101%	44	100%	43	98%

Latin 11

Range	1968 Totals	%	1969 Totals	%	1970 Totals	%	1971 Totals	%
100-90	2	4%	9	16%	12	26%	9	24%
89-80	11	24%	6	11%	10	21%	10	27%
79-70	9	20%	14	25%	14	30%	11	29%
69-65	12	26%	14	25%	7	15%	4	10%
Fail	12	26%	13	23%	4	9%	3	8%
	46	100%	56	100%	47	101%	37	98%

Spanish 111

Range	1968 Totals	%	1969 Totals	%	1970 Totals	%	1971 Totals	%
100-90	5	42%	2	22%	4	50%	5	71%
89-80	1	8%	–	–	2	25%	2	29%
79-70	4	33%	3	33%	1	13%		
69-65	1	8%	2	22%	1	13%		
Fail	1	8%	2	22%	–	–		
	12	99%	9	99%	8	101%	7	100%

Biology

Range	1968 Totals	%	1969 Totals	%	1970 Totals	%	1971 Totals	%
100-90	19	14%	5	5%	22	17%	20	17%
89-80	43	33%	14	14%	28	21%	38	32%
79-70	33	25%	24	23%	37	28%	39	33%
69-65	18	14%	14	14%	15	11%	8	7%
Fail	19	14%	45	44%	30	23%	14	12%
	132	100%	102	100%	132	100%	119	101%

Chemistry

Range	1968 Totals	%	1969 Totals	%	1970 Totals	%	1971 Totals	%
100-90	19	24%	22	30%	14	19%	32	43%
89-80	30	38%	27	37%	32	44%	26	35%
79-70	19	24%	17	23%	21	29%	10	13%
69-65	5	6%	4	5%	3	4%	3	4%
Fail	6	8%	3	4%	2	3%	4	5%
	79	100%	73	99%	72	99%	75	100%

Physics

Range	1968 Totals	%	1969 Totals	%	1970 Totals	%	1971 Totals	%
100-90	17	38%	22	39%	8	21%	9	25%
89-80	18	40%	23	41%	18	47%	9	25%
79-70	7	16%	9	16%	11	29%	13	36%
69-65	1	2%	1	2%	-	-	3	8%
Fail	2	4%	1	2%	1	3%	2	6%
	45	100%	56	100%	38	100%	36	100%

Typing 1

Range	1968 Totals	%	1969 Totals	%	1970 Totals	%	1971 Totals	%
100-90	9	15%	8	12%	6	10%	2	4%
89-80	11	18%	17	25%	20	32%	8	15%
79-70	12	20%	13	19%	17	27%	18	35%
69-65	12	20%	7	10%	11	18%	5	10%
Fail	16	27%	23	34%	8	13%	19	36%
	60	100%	68	100%	62	100%	52	100%

Business Math

Range	1968 Totals	%	1969 Totals	%	1970 Totals	%	1971 Totals	%
100-90	–		2	13%	1	4%	3	15%
89-80	7	29%	5	31%	7	27%	6	30%
79-70	4	17%	3	19%	12	46%	2	10%
69-65	6	25%	3	19%	2	8%	4	20%
Fail	7	29%	3	19%	4	15%	5	25%
	24	100%	16	101%	26	100%	20	100%

Business Law

Range	1968 Totals	%	1969 Totals	%	1970 Totals	%	1971 Totals	%
100-90	–		–		–		–	
89-80	1	6%	–		3	27%	2	13%
79-70	7	44%	9	39%	5	45%	2	13%
69-65	3	19%	8	35%	3	27%	7	44%
Fail	5	31%	6	26%	–		5	31%
	16	100%	23	100%	11	99%	16	100%

Shorthand 11 & Transcription

Range	1968 Totals	%	1969 Totals	%	1970 Totals	%	1971 Totals	%
100-90	2	8%	2	10%	4	29%	4	26%
89-80	5	21%	6	30%	2	14%	4	26%
79-70	5	21%	3	15%	3	21%	3	20%
69-65	3	13%	3	15%	1	7%	1	6%
Fail	9	38%	6	30%	4	29%	3	20%
	24	101%	20	100%	14	100%	15	98%

Bibliography on Flexible Scheduling

Allen, Dwight W., "Element of Scheduling a Flexible Curriculum," *Journal of Secondary Education,* Vol. 38 (November, 1963), pp. 84-91.

Allen, Dwight W., "First Steps in Developing a More Flexible Schedule," *Bulletin of the National Association of Secondary School Principals,* Vol. 46 (May, 1963), pp. 34-36.

Anderson, Robert H., "Organizing Groups for Instruction," *Individualizing Instruction,* NSSE Yrbk. '61, Part 1. Chicago: University of Chicago Press, 1962, pp. 239-264.

Austin, David, and Noble Gividen, *The High School Principal and Staff Develop the Master Schedule.* New York: Bureau of Publications, Teachers College, Columbia University, 1960.

Beggs, David W. and Edward Buffie, eds., *Independent Study.* Indiana University Press, 1966.

Beggs, David W., *Team Teaching.* Indiana University Press, 1964.

Beggs, David, *Decatur-Lakeview High School: A Practical Application of the Trump Plan.* Englewood Cliffs, N.J.: Prentice-Hall, Inc., 1964.

Benthall, Marguerite S. (Principal, Alexis I. Du Pont High School, Greenvale, Deleware), *"Flexible Scheduling: Secondary Education Comes of Age."* Unpublished article, p. 12.

Bishop, Lloyd K., *Individualizing Educational Systems.* New York: Harper and Row, 1971, p. 276.

Boyan, Norman, "Team Teaching, A Theme with Variations," Stanford University, 1962.

Boyan, Norman J., "The Role of the Principal in Developing Greater Flexibility in High School Education," *Bulletin of the National Association of Secondary School Principals,* Vol. 46 (May, 1962), pp. 36-42.

Brown, B. Frank, "The Nongraded High School," Englewood Cliffs, N.J.: Prentice-Hall, Inc., 1963.

Brunner, Jerome S., *The Process of Education.* Harvard University Press, 1965.

Brunner, Jerome S., *Toward a Theory of Instruction.* Harvard University Press, 1967.

Bush, Robert N., "A New Design for High School Education: Assuming a Flexible Schedule," *Bulletin of the National Association of Secondary School Principals,* Vol. 46 (May, 1962), pp. 30-34.

Bush, Robert N., and Dwight W. Allen, "Flexible Scheduling for What?" *Journal of Secondary Education,* Vol. 36, No. 6, October, 1961.

Bush, R.N., and Dwight W. Allen, *A New Design for High School Education: Assuming a Flexible Schedule.* New York: McGraw-Hill, 1964.

Bush, R.N., and D.W. Allen, "Flexible Scheduling," *Bulletin of the National Association of Secondary School Principals,* Vol 47 (May, 1963), pp. 73-98.

Cawelti, Gordon, "Does Innovation Make Any Difference?" *Nation's Schools,* Vol. 82, No. 5, November, 1968.

Coombs, Arthur Jr., Robert F. Madgic, Robert V. Oakford, Toshio Sato, and Ray Talbert. *Variable Modular Scheduling.* New York: Benziger, Inc., 1971.

Devilboss, Wilber, "Criteria of a Good Master Schedule," *National Association of Secondary School Principals Bulletin,* Vol. 31, No. 149, November, 1947.

Educational Facilities Laboratory, Ford Foundation, "Profiles of Significant High Schools," 1962.

Ellsworth, R.E., and H.D. Wagener, *The School Library: Facilities for Independent Study in the Secondary School.* Educational Facilities Laboratories, N.Y., 1963.

Engle, F.S., "Large Group Instruction Can Work." *Nation's Schools,* 70: 70-71, October, 1962.

Etzioni, Amitai., *A Comparative Analysis of Complex Organization.* New York: The Free Press, 1961.

Evans, Marvin. *A Comparative Study of Secondary School Independent Study Programs: Final Report.* Report No. BR-6-8389. Eugene, Oregon: University of Oregon, 1968 (ERIC ED 019 705).

Evanston Township High School Annual Report, "What is Modular Scheduling?" 1967.

"Flexible Modular Scheduling," Post Workshop Report; Bureau of Curriculum Instruction, Division of Elementary and Secondary Education, Department of Education, Tallahassee, Florida, January, 1970.

"The Flexibly Scheduled School of 1980," a Report of the National Seminar on Modular Flexible Scheduling, an I/D/E/A Occasional Paper, 1971.

Frinks, Marshall L., and Donald K. Sharpes, "Key Elements: Time–Space–Personnel," *Florida Schools*, Nov.-Dec. 1969.

Gladstone, Igor, M., "Modified Scheduling and Foreign Language." *NASSP Bulletin.* November, 1966, pp. 121-127.

Glatthorn, Allan A., *Learning in the Small Group,* Institute for Development of Educational Activities, I/D/E/A, Dayton, Ohio, 1966.

Gorton, Richard A. (Principal, Madison High School, Madison, Wisconsin), "Parental Resistance to Modular Scheduling," in *Contemporary Concers,* 1969, pp. 392-439.

Grod, Robert R., "A Realistic Look at the Flexible Schedule." *The Clearing House,* March, 1969, pp. 425-429.

Gross, Robert, and Robert Watt, "Staff Involvement and Structural Change," *Journal of Secondary Education,* March, 1969, Vol. 44, No. 3, pp. 112-115.

Haugo, John E., "A Comparative Analysis of Two Plans of High School Organization for Instruction: Modular versus Traditional," unpublished Ph.D. dissertation, University of Minnesota, 1968.

Hausken, Chester A. *A Study of Achievement in Spokane High Schools with Different Organizational Patterns.* Spokane, Washington: Research Report, Spokane Public Schools, 1967.

Heller, Melvin, James E. Smith, and Bettye Belford, "The New Look in Class Schedules, Teacher Responsibilities, and Student Programs," *School Management,* Vol. 5, No. 10, October, 1961.

Heller, Robert W., "Informal Organization and Perceptions of the Organizational Climate of Schools," *Journal of Educational Research,* Vol. 61, No. 9, May-June, 1968.

Hicken, James E., "An Assessment of a Senior High School Modular Scheduling Program," Dade County Public Schools, Miami, Florida, June, 1968, p. 19.

Hilfiker, Leo R., "The Relationship of School System Innovativeness to Selected Dimensions of Interpersonal Behavior in Eight School Systems," *Technical Report No. 70, Models for Planned Educational Change Project.* Madison, Wisconsin, University of Wisconsin, January, 1969 (ERIC ED 029 808).

Hock, Louise E., "What, Why, and How of Classroom Grouping for Effective Learning," *Educational Leadership,* 18:420-24, April, 1961.

Johnson, Howard, "Flexibility in the Secondary School," *National Association of Secondary School Principals Bulletin,* Vol. 53, No. 339, October, 1969.

Johnson, Robert H., "An Extensive Study of Team Teaching and Schedule Modification," *NASSP Bulletin,* 44:78-93, January, 1960.

Johnson, Robert H., "Jefferson County, Colorado Completes Three-Year Study of Staffing, Changing Class Size, Programming, and Scheduling." *NASSP,* 45:57-58, January, 1961.

Johnson, Lobb, and Patterson, "Continued Study of Class Size, Team Teaching and Scheduling in Eight High Schools in Jefferson County, Colorado," *NASSP*, January 1959, pp. 99-103.

Keim, W.P., *Evaluation of a New Design for Secondary Educational Excellence.* Wilmington, Delaware: John Dickinson High School Monograph, 1969.

Lebb, M. Delbert, "A Basis for First Steps in Flexible Scheduling," *Journal of Secondary Education,* Vol. 36, No. 6, October, 1961, pp. 367-70.

Leigh, Thomas G., "Big Opportunities in Small Schools Through Flexible Modular Scheduling," *Journal of Secondary Education,* Vol. 42, No. 4, April, 1967.

Lisonbee, Lorenzo, "Large Group Teaching," *Science Teacher,* 29:33-35, February, 1962.

McNassor, Don, "The Teaching Team Plan for High School Education," Claremont Graduate School, an unpublished report, 1961.

Mager, Robert F., *Preparing Instructional Objectives.* Feardon Publishers, Palo Alto, California, 1962.

Mager, Robert F., "Preparing Objectives for Programmed Instruction," Varion Association, 1962.

Manlove, D.C., and D.W. Beggs, *Flexible Scheduling: Bold New Venture.* Bloomington, Indiana: Indiana University Press, 1965.

Marcum, Laverne, R., *Organizational Climate and the Adoption of Educational Innovation.* United State Office of Education Project OEG 4 7 078 119 2901, Utah State University, 1968.

Panwitt, Barbara S., "Report on Five years of Projects, Including . . . Large and Small Group Instruction," *NASSP Bulletin,* 45:244-48, January, 1961.

Petrequin, Gaynor, *Individualized Learning Through Modular-Flexible Scheduling.* New York: McGraw-Hill Co., 1968.

Petrequin, Gaynor, and William Tapfer, "Hand Generation and Hand Loading of a Modular-Variable Schedule," I/D/E/A Scheduling Manual Development Edition, Institute for Development of Educational Activities, Inc., 1970.

Read, Ed, and John Drakovich, "The Continuous Progress Plan," Brigham Young University Press, 1963.

Richardson, D.H., "Independent Study: What Difference Does It Make?" *National Association of Secondary School Principals Bulletin,* Vol. 51, No. 320, September, 1967.

Shaplin, Judson T., and Henry F. Olds, Jr., eds, *Team Teaching.* New York: Harper and Row, 1964.

Silberman, Charles., *Crisis in the Classroom.* New York: Random House, 1970.

Singer, Ira, "Reducing the Research-to-Practice Gap," Audiovisual Instruction, an unpublished report, November, 1963.

Singer, Ira, "Survey of Staff Utilization Practices in Six States," *NASSP,* 1962.

Speckhard, Gerald P., "Evaluating the Modular Schedule,"*North Central Association Quarterly,* Vol. XLI, No. 4, Spring, 1967.

Speckhard, Gerald and Alenn Bracht, "An Evaluation of the Education Program of a High School Using a Modular Schedule: A Follow-Up Study." U.S. Department of Health, Education, and Welfare, Washington, D.C., ERIC ED 025 850.

Swenson, Gardner, and Donald Keys, *Providing for Flexibility in Scheduling and Instruction.* Englewood Cliffs, N.J.:Prentice-Hall, Inc., 1966.

Symposium: "Flexible Scheduling: An Appraisal to Individualizing Instruction in Secondary Schools," *Journal of Secondary Education,* Vol. 36 (October, 1961), pp. 336-384.

Symposium: "New Designs for the Secondary School Schedule," *California Journal of Secondary School Education,* Vol. 35 (February, 1960), pp. 91-134.

Symposium: "New Opportunities for Expertness—Team Teaching and Flexible Scheduling," *Journal of Secondary Education,* Vol. 37 (October, 1962) pp. 340-382. The conference is summarized in articles by Frank B. Lindsay, Lester W. Nelson, Harold Howe, Arthur B. King, B. Frank Brown, and Archibald B. Shaw. (Conference held at Stanford University in the summer of 1962.)

Trump, J. Lloyd, "Flexible Scheduling—Fad or Fundamental," *Phi Delta Kappa,* May, 1963.

Trump, J. Lloyd, and Dorsey Bayham, *Focus on Change, Guide to Better Schools,* Rand and McNally, 1961.

Trump, J. Lloyd, "Images of the Future,"*NASSP,* 1959.

Trump, J. Lloyd, "New Directions in Scheduling and Use of Staff in the High School," *California Journal of Secondary* Education, Vol. 33 (October, 1958), pp. 362-372.

Trump, J. Lloyd, "Planning a Team-Teaching Program,"*NASSP,* 1963.

Trump, J. Lloyd, "Quality Education of the Future,"*NASSP,* January, 1962.

U.S. Department of Health, Education, and Welfare. A Report Concerning the Summer Workshop on Modular Scheduling: An Activity of the Title III Project, The Use of Modular Scheduling in Curriculum Improvement. Washington, D.C., ERIC ED 022 241.

Vorlop, Frederic, and T.J. Sheridan. *A Study to Determine Achievement Progress of Delavan-Darien High School Students During the 1968-69 School Year.* Delavan, Wisconsin: Delavan High School Report, 1969.

Warden, Eric and Paula B. Leidich, *An Adaptation of Variable Scheduling to the Program of a Small Junior High School.* Michigan University: Ann Arbor, 1969, p. 44.

Westby-Gibson, Dorothy, *Grouping Students for Improved Instruction.* Englewood Cliffs, N.J.: Prentice-Hall, Inc., 1966.

Wiley, Deane, and Lloyd Bishop, *The Flexibly Scheduled High School.* West Nyack, New York: Parker Publishing Co., Inc., 1968.

Wilhelms, Fred, "The Curriculum and Individual Differences," NSSE Yrbk. 1961. Part 1. *Individualizing Instruction.*, Chicago Press, 1962, pp. 239-264.

Index

F

Flexible Modular Scheduling, 19, 24, 32, 35-
  36, 38-39, 47-50, 55, 57, 91, 106, 111,
  117, 120, 121-122, 126-127, 129-130,
  138, 140, 142, 152, 156, 159
Flexibility, 24, 26, 28, 38, 46, 87
Floating Periods, 41
Ford Foundation, 43
Free Times (See Unstructured Time)
Foreign Language, 22, 26, 33-34, 89, 104,
  118-119, 153

G

Generalized Academic Simulation Program
  (GASP), 43, 45
Group Counseling, 121
Guidance, 38, 96-97, 119, 120, 121-122, 128

H

Hand Scheduling, 47
Hansen, Burdette, P., 147-148
Holtz, Robert, 43
Home Economics, 22, 35, 118

I

IBM, 95
I/D/E/A Institute, 130
Independent Study (IS), 57-58, 150-152, 163
Individualized Instruction, 27-28, 38, 93, 115,
  117, 163
Informal Education, 158
Industrial Arts, 118
In-Service, 125, 136
Institute of Administrative Research, 31
Instructional Resource Center (Materials Cen-
  ter), 38, 117, 163

L

Laboratories (Labs), 38, 58, 71, 104, 118-119,
  163-164
Large Group Instruction, 27-30, 34, 58, 61, 71,
  78, 84, 102-104, 119, 164
Learning Activities Packages, 57
Little Falls High School, 31
Lock-step, 20
Lunch, 87, 93, 164, 185

M

Marshall (John) High School, 44, 48
Master Schedule, 40, 43, 46, 65-67, 70, 72,
  77, 79, 83-84, 89, 92-93, 95, 97-98,
  100-102
Math, 22, 34, 57, 118, 150
Measurement Research Corp., 147-148
Mechanical Drawing, 35
Melbourne High School, Florida, 130
Mini-Courses, 107, 119, 129, 164

Mixed Groups, 84
Mode of Instruction, 28, 34, 40, 55, 58, 59,
  61, 69, 70, 72, 83, 104, 164
Mods, 23-26, 51-52, 58, 60, 69, 79, 84, 89,
  91-92, 106, 113, 118, 120, 164
Mods, Length of, 25-26
Mod Blocking, 88, 89
Module (See Mods)
Monotony, 20

N

Newsweek, 158
Northeast High School, Florida, 147, 158,
  176-187
Norwich Senior High School, N. Y., 35, 47, 49,
  60, 115, 126, 128-129, 130-138, 140,
  142, 148, 188-196
Nova High School, Florida, 52, 130

O

Oakford, Robert, 43-44
Open Labs (See Laboratories)
Orchestra, 36

P

Parents, 122, 158-159, 186
Paternalism of Schools, 37
Periods, 20
Petrequin, Gaynor, 44-45
Phases (See Modes of Instruction)
Physical Education, 22, 35, 100
Principal, 66, 75, 83, 126-127
Priority Cards, 67, 69-70, 82-85
Program Alternatives, 20, 38, 42
Public Relations, 137-138

Q

Quiet Study, 37, 115, 164

R

Regents, 153-156
Regular Class, 31, 58, 71, 90, 102, 104, 164
Research Based Work, 32, 117
Resistance Factors, 127-128, 129
Resource Centers, 38, 92, 115, 117, 164, 186
Rotating Scheduling, 38, 41, 120

S

Scatter Scheduling, 89-90
Scheduling, 32, 42
Schedule and Adjustments, 48, 91, 94, 100,
  104
Scheduling – Balancing, 113
Scheduling – Compromises, 48, 65, 91, 173
Scheduling – Cost, 46, 48, 108, 183-184